Making Stained Glass Panels

Michael Johnston

Photographs by Alan Wycheck

STACKPOLE
BOOKS

Copyright © 2010 by Stackpole Books

Published by
STACKPOLE BOOKS
5067 Ritter Road
Mechanicsburg, PA 17055
www.stackpolebooks.com

Printed in the United States of America

10   9   8   7   6   5   4   3   2

First edition

Cover design by Tessa J. Sweigert

Library of Congress Cataloging-in-Publication Data

Johnston, Michael, 1947–
 Making stained glass panels / Michael Johnston ; photographs by Alan Wycheck.
  p. cm.
 ISBN 978-0-8117-3638-1
 1. Glass craft. 2. Glass painting and staining. I. Title.
 TT298.J655 2010
 748.5—dc22
                                            2009049984

contents

acknowledgments

This book is dedicated to my wife of twenty-five years, Jane Inzana Johnston, who has supported the notion of me "toiling" in a profession that has seemed a whole lot more like recreation than a real job. She's the best!

As this book began to develop, it became clear that many people would play important roles in bringing it to completion.

Foremost, I thank Mark Allison and Kathryn Fulton from Stackpole Books for their expert guidance, from the conceptualization of the project to the very end.

Thanks also to photographer extraordinaire Alan Wycheck. His keen ability to see things most people miss and capture them with his Nikon played a vital role in the presentation of the book.

Great appreciation is due my loyal friends and colleagues from Rainbow Vision Stained Glass: Nan Maund, Lynn Haunstein, and Lee Summers. In addition to contributing designs and finished panels for the Stained Glass Panel Gallery, they all ably assisted in many other aspects of the book's development.

My three high-tech children, Craig, Melissa, and Ashley, were instrumental in the typing and editing stages as well as offering countless suggestions about better ways to clarify the instruction.

I also thank the thousands of students who have come through the doors of Rainbow Vision looking for help in building the perfect stained glass window. Your support has been wonderful.

Lastly, I salute my grandsons, Jackson, Conner, Carter, and Brady. May some of you develop an interest to carry on the stained glass torch.

introduction

I remember as a youngster sitting in the solemn confines of St. Francis of Assisi Church and being mesmerized by the gorgeous stained glass that was electrified by the sun. There were ten large windows in all, each one telling its own story from the New Testament. There was certainly a lot to look at: human figures, animals, background scenery, and the colors—oh, the colors. After twelve years of window gazing during my somewhat regular attendance, I had committed a lot to memory and developed quite an appreciation for old St. Francis.

Twenty years passed before I picked up my first glass cutter, fashioned a few rather primitive-looking projects, and resumed my stained glass journey, a journey that has proven to be a wonderful way to travel through life.

In this book, we have taken the teaching methods used in our studio for the past twenty-five years and put them in a cohesive learning plan with hundreds of accompanying photographs and detailed step-by-step instructions for building a beautiful stained glass window panel. There are two primary methods for building panels: using traditional lead channels, or cames, and the copper foil, or Tiffany, method. Both methods are described completely in this book to help you master them both.

The featured project in the book is a classic design featuring a double arched border with repeating arches in the background. The center motif is a $10^{5}/8$-inch circle with seven different design options to choose from. By selecting one design over another, you can achieve a significantly different look. We have also included faceted jewels in the border as well as in the upper star.

The project uses all of the techniques needed to build a wide variety of panels. It is intended to be challenging but not overwhelming. If you are new to the craft, we have included brief primers in cutting glass, soldering copper foil, and cutting and soldering lead. I recommend that you first build one or two of the panel's center circles for practice, following the instructions in chapters 4 and 5. This will prepare you for the successful completion of the larger panel.

There is, however, one additional skill that you need to bring to the workbench: patience. Read all of the instructions and take your time. It is not a race; there is no prize for finishing first. This project might be a significant part of your stained glass legacy, so build it well.

1

A Good Work Environment

AS YOUR INTEREST IN STAINED GLASS BLOS-
soms, you will discover that you are spending
a great deal of time in your glass shop. You will
want some creature comforts. Four elements greatly
contribute to a comfortable and efficient shop:

- good light source
- sturdy work table
- nearby water source
- adequate ventilation

All aspects of stained glass making (cutting, foiling,
soldering, and so on) involve a need for precision, and
the better you see, the better the final product will be.
A two- or four-bulb fluorescent light hanging over a
workbench is generally adequate.

A workbench should be sturdy and at a comfortable
height. If you are of average height, a tabletop approximately 34 inches from the floor will probably work
well. Plywood construction is ideal, and a size of
30 inches by 72 inches will accommodate most projects. A piece of fire-resistant fiberboard about 2 feet by
3 feet in size can be placed on the plywood tabletop.

Homasote has a firm surface with a slight spring,
which makes it perfect for glass cutting (plywood by
itself is a bit rigid). Pushpins and nails are easily secured
in homasote, and soldering is easier and safer because of
its fire resistance. Homasote used to be readily available
at building supply stores but is harder to find now. You
might have to call around to find it or settle for a substi-
tute product.

1

In addition to providing a handy place to wash up, a nearby sink will make it easy to clean the project at various stages. Any size basin can work, but one with an opening of 12 by 20 inches or larger is ideal. Use a screen strainer to prevent sand and other debris from making its way into the drainpipes.

Set up shop in the area that is convenient to you based on the space you have available. You will probably have only so many options and often must do the best you can. Ideally, you will want an area that has good ventilation—especially when you are soldering. If this is not possible, use a small table fan on your workbench or purchase a smoke absorber, available at stained glass supply stores. You can also experiment with opening adjacent doors and windows to create a cross breeze.

In addition to the shop features listed here, several other items will be very useful:
- bench brush and dustpan, for cleaning up glass shards and other debris
- storage bins for sheets of glass
- cabinet for chemicals and tools
- comfortable stool
- radio or MP3 or CD player
- multi-receptacle surge suppressor with an LED light. This will allow you to have several electrical items plugged in at once. And the light will act as a visual reminder to turn off your soldering iron at the end of each work session.

STAINED GLASS SAFETY

Stained glass is generally a very safe craft, and by adopting the safety precautions listed here, you will greatly reduce the likelihood of injuries and health problems.

- The most common injury that occurs with stained glass is a cut finger. Prevention includes careful handling of the glass and frequent brushing of your work area to eliminate shards and specks of glass. If you do get a cut, tend to it right away by applying an antiseptic and band aid. Keep these items at close hand in your shop.

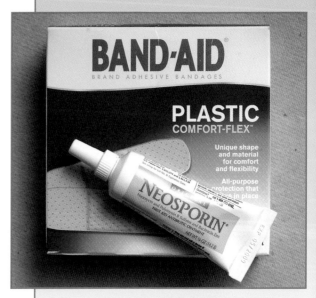

- Never eat, drink, or smoke while engaged in any of the steps in making stained glass items.

- Be careful and use common sense when working with lead cames and solder. Generally, stained glass crafters are exposed to only very low levels of lead while building their projects. Make sure any open wounds are bandaged and that you thoroughly wash your hands after working with lead or solder.
- Wear closed-toed shoes at all times to avoid glass injuries to your feet.
- Do not allow pets in your work area.
- Use rubber gloves when working with patinas and etching creams. These substances can cause chemical burns on exposed skin and can be harmful if absorbed into the bloodstream.
- Always wear safety glasses when cutting or grinding glass. When using an electric grinder, though, be sure to also use the eye shield that attaches to the machine. Safety glasses alone are not sufficient, as ground debris will get on your face and cause skin irritation.
- Use care when handling large sheets of glass. Grip the sheet by its top edge and move it slowly to avoid jarring. Never hold a large sheet of glass horizontally because it might crack from the strain. Never try to catch a falling sheet of glass—let it go and move quickly out of the way.

- To avoid burns, use a heavy-duty stand to house your soldering iron when it's not in use.
- Take care that the cord of the soldering iron does not become entangled in the spirals of the stand. This will prevent damage to the cord and possible electrical problems.
- When soldering, position your head so that you are not directly breathing in fumes from the flux.
- Always wash your hands thoroughly after working in any phase of stained glass construction.
- Avoid soldering in tight spaces with little ventilation. Create some airflow with a small fan or open windows. Smoke absorbers are also available in most stained glass supply shops.

- Scraps of lead came should be recycled. If you do not have access to a recycler, ask the store where you purchased your lead to take it off your hands.
- Consider placing a piece of rubber-backed carpet under the area where you will be cutting. It will provide a comfortable cushion to stand on and it can save those pieces of glass that slip off the table.

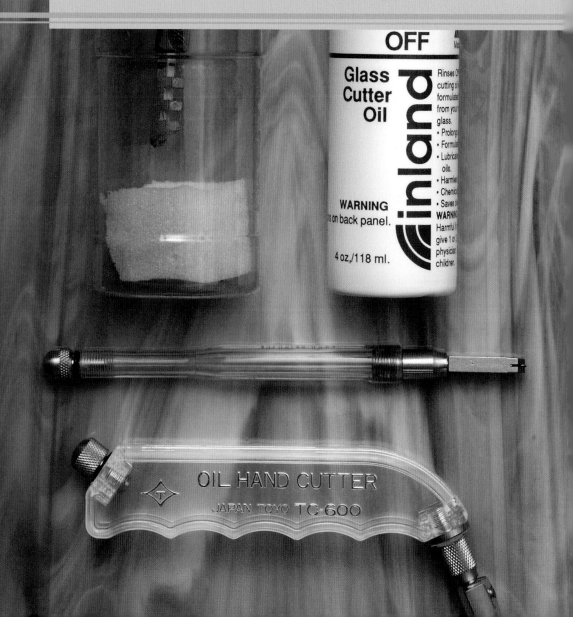

2

Equipment and Materials

IF YOU HAVE BEEN WORKING WITH STAINED glass you probably already have most of the tools necessary to complete a panel in either lead or copper foil. And, depending on the projects you have completed, a lot of the supplies might also be in your workshop.

This chapter lists and describes all of the items used in chapters 7 through 9 for building your panel. These items are also included on a checklist at the end of the chapter.

5

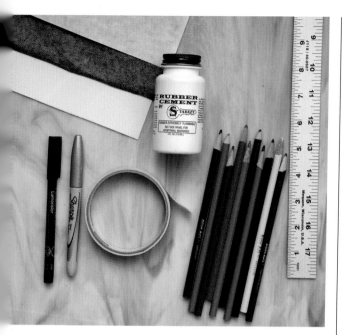

- **Conventional glass cutter.** Available with a steel or carbide wheel (shown in a jar that contains a sponge soaked in cutting oil).
- **Upright acrylic cutter.** This pencil-shaped cutter usually comes with a carbide wheel and is self-oiling.
- **Pistol cutter.** The pistol cutter's shape makes it comfortable to hold and allows you to use the larger muscles in your hand to apply pressure to the glass. This results in less hand fatigue during extended cutting sessions. Most pistol cutters are self oiling.
- **Cutting oil.** Used to cool the cutting wheel, reducing friction on the glass during a score. Oil also lubricates the wheel, allowing it to turn freely.

- **Tracing paper.** Translucent paper allows lines from the original pattern to show through so they can be traced.
- **Carbon paper.** Inky blue or black paper allows the design to be transferred onto oak tag.
- **Oak tag.** About as think as a manila file folder; used to help you assemble glass pieces prior to soldering.
- **Colored pencils.** Used to designate glass colors on paper pattern pieces.
- **Rubber cement.** Attaches paper pattern templates onto glass.
- **Glass markers.** For writing numbers on glass and drawing pattern shapes.
- **Cork-backed ruler.** For measuring and cutting straight edges in glass. The cork prevents the ruler from slipping during cutting.
- **Masking tape.** Attaches patterns during tracing.

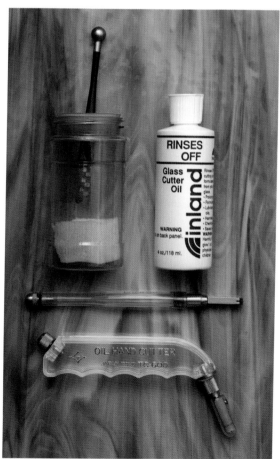

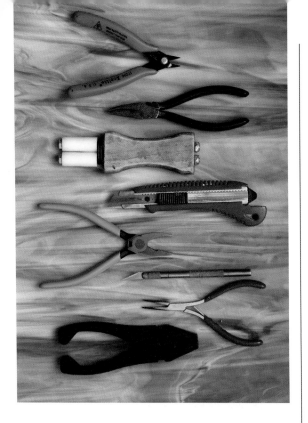

PRO TIP ✔

If you visit a local stained glass supply store you'll notice that there are lots of choices in tools. Our experience over the years has made us firm believers that better tools, though more expensive, are more effective in getting the job done and much more durable.

Whatever your approach, the three most important tools are the following:

- Glass Cutter
- Breaking/grozing pliers
- Soldering iron

If your resources are limited, buy the best of these tools that you can afford.

- **Wire cutters.** Used for cutting wire hooks and hangers.
- **Needle-nose pliers.** Used in repair work and to hold pieces of wire during soldering.
- **Foil finisher.** Used to burnish the edges of foil on glass.
- **Utility knife.** Used in the repair of leaded windows.
- **Breaking/grozing pliers.** Your main glass-breaking tool; also used for grozing (shaping glass), these are sometimes called "combo pliers."
- **Craft knife.** Used to trim foil and create foil patches.
- **Small needle-nose pliers.** Used to hold small wire hooks.
- **Running pliers.** Used to separate glass along a score line. The upper jaw has a node on each side and the lower jaw has a node in the middle. When the pliers are centered on a score line, squeezing them causes the glass to "run" and separate.

- **Lead pliers.** Also called dykes, these are used to cut lead came (two different styles are shown at far left and far right).
- **Lead knife.** Also used to cut lead came.
- **Hammer.** Used to drive nails into plywood to hold glass and leads in place; also used to tap pieces of glass into pieces of lead.
- **Horseshoe nails.** Flat nails used to hold leads and glass in place.

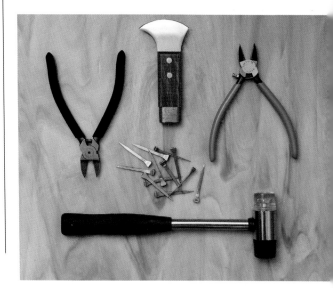

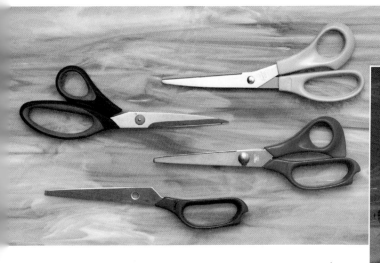

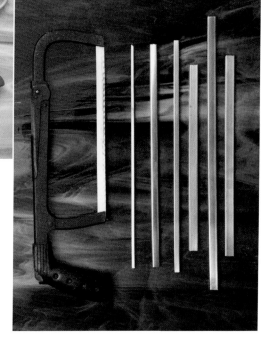

Pattern shears, in general, are special three-bladed shears that remove a thin strip of the paper pattern; this reduces each pattern piece just enough so that when copper foil is applied or the glass is inserted into lead channel, the pattern returns to its original size.

- **Lead shears.** These remove a little *more* than $1/16$ inch of the pattern (shown with gray handles).
- **Foil shears.** These remove a little *less* than $1/16$ inch of the pattern (black handles).
- **Combination shears.** These shears have interchangeable blades for lead or foil (blue handles).

- **Lead board.** Made of $3/8$-inch or thicker plywood, this board has wood strips on two sides that form a 90-degree angle.
- **Lead stretcher.** This metal device is mounted to a workbench; it allows you to stretch and strengthen lead strips.
- **Brass brush.** Used to remove tarnish from old or oxidized lead.
- **Lead cames.** Generally, these come in 6-foot strips. U-channel leads have a single channel; H-channel leads have two channels. Common sizes range from $1/16$ inch to $1/4$ inch.
- **Other metal cames.** Zinc, copper, and brass are options for framing a large stained glass panel. They are much harder than lead and do not stretch. They are available in sizes ranging from $1/8$ inch to $3/4$ inch. A **hacksaw** is the tool of choice for cutting these metals.

- **Homasote board.** An ideal work surface because it is portable, fire resistant, and soft enough for pins to be inserted. It also provides a slight cushion for cutting glass. Liquids will bead up on it, so a spilled jar of flux is not a big problem. A homasote board about 24 inches by 36 inches is ideal.
- **Bench brush.** Used for keeping your work area free of glass shards, solder balls, and so on.
- **Foiling machine.** This machine is mounted on a piece of wood so it can be clamped to your workbench. It allows you to attach foil to the glass pieces evenly and quickly.
- **Fid.** The red plastic tool is a fid, used for burnishing foil to the glass.
- **Foil finisher.** The wooden-handled tool with two white rollers is used to burnish two sides of the foiled glass simultaneously.

- **Cement.** Used to strengthen and weatherproof leaded windows.
- **Whiting.** Calcium carbonate powder is used to harden cement and clean up a leaded window.
- **Scrub brush.** Used to apply cement under lead channels and polish them.
- **Wood pick.** To remove excess cement from the window.
- **Patina.** Chemical that reacts to solder, turning it a different color.
- **Finishing wax.** Applied as the final step, the wax adds a protective coating to the glass and solder, resulting in an attractive shine.
- **Carborundum stone.** Used to remove burrs or sharp edges from the cut glass.

- **Electric grinder.** Has a water-cooled diamond drum that smoothes the edges of cut glass.
- **Steel wool.** To shine zinc and remove patina.
- **Nylon scrubbing pad.** Used to remove the numbers you've written on the glass.
- **Tinned copper wire.** Available in several gauges, the wire has many uses, including making hooks, adding reinforcement, and so on.
- **Foam sponges.** To apply patinas.
- **Rubber gloves.** For hand protection when applying patina or other harsh chemicals.

- **Soldering iron.** Melts the solder onto the panel, connecting the cames or the copper foil.
- **Safety stand.** Holds the iron; a highly recommended safety device.
- **Flux.** A chemical that removes oxidation from various metals, allowing solder to flow smoothly. Most are either liquid or gel.
- **Flux brush.** Used for applying flux to a metal.
- **Flux bottle holder.** Prevents the flux bottle from spilling.
- **Solder.** The preferred solder used in stained glass is a mixture of 60 percent tin and 40 percent lead (called 60/40 solder). Always use a good-quality solder that's made for stained glass.

PRO TIP ✔

When deciding what soldering iron to buy, consider these three important features:

1 The iron should be 80–100 watts.

2 The iron should have temperature control capability. Some irons have this feature built in; others require a separate rheostat.

3 The iron should have a chisel-shaped tip, $1/4$ inch to $1/2$ inch wide.

- **Oak framing.** Available in six-foot pieces-used to make frames for stained glass panels.
- **Oak corner blocks.** Used to join sides of wooden frames.
- **Brass hangers.** These can be fastened to the sides of wooden frames; lengths of chain are then attached for hanging.

CHECKLIST: BUILDING A STAINED GLASS PANEL

Items marked with an (L) are for leaded panels; items with a (C) are for copper foil panels.

Tools

- [ ] Soldering Iron
- [ ] Iron Stand
- [ ] Glass Cutter
- [ ] Breaking/Grozing Pliers
- [ ] Grinder
- [ ] Carborundum Stone
- [ ] Pattern Shears
- [ ] Glass Square
- [ ] Running Pliers
- [ ] Foiling Machine (C)
- [ ] Foil Finisher (C)
- [ ] Fids (C)
- [ ] Craft Knife (C)
- [ ] Utility Knife
- [ ] Needle-nose Pliers
- [ ] Wire Cutters
- [ ] Flux Brush
- [ ] Lead Cutters (L)
- [ ] Lead Knife (L)

Chemicals

- [ ] Cutter Oil
- [ ] Flux
- [ ] Flux Remover
- [ ] Patina (C)
- [ ] Finishing Compound (C)
- [ ] Rubber Cement
- [ ] Cement (L)
- [ ] Whiting (L)

Supplies

- [ ] 60/40 Solder
- [ ] Lead (L)
- [ ] $7/32$-inch Copper Foil (C)
- [ ] Tracing Paper
- [ ] Carbon Paper
- [ ] Oak Tag
- [ ] Masking Tape
- [ ] Soft Sponge
- [ ] Window Glass
- [ ] Assorted Glass
- [ ] Steel Wool
- [ ] 18- or 20-gauge Wire
- [ ] Zinc (C)

Miscellaneous

- [ ] Scissors
- [ ] Layout Strips/Pushpins (C)
- [ ] Cork-backed Ruler
- [ ] Colored Pencils
- [ ] Homasote Board (C)
- [ ] Safety Glasses
- [ ] Markers
- [ ] Sponges
- [ ] Towels
- [ ] Bench Brush
- [ ] Scrub Brush (L)
- [ ] Plywood Board (L)
- [ ] Hammer (L)

3

Glass Cutting Primer

THE MORE ACCURATELY YOU ARE ABLE TO CUT the glass, the less grozing, grinding, and fitting you will have to do, and ultimately, the nicer the finished project will be. Although glass grinders allow you to fashion a circle from a square in a minute or two, this type of shortcut is not what the craft is about. As a crafter in the art of stained glass, you will want to become adept at cutting glass.

Nearly thirty years have passed since I scored and broke my first piece of glass, but I confess that glass cutting continues to be a pleasure. I marvel at the way a barely visible scratch in the glass can result in a perfectly cut-out shape. And the whole glass experience is so much more enjoyable when the glass actually breaks the way you want it to.

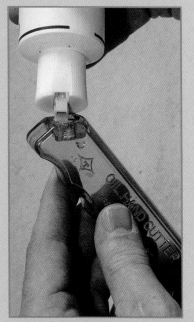

Over the past two decades, more than three thousand students have attended our classes, and nearly every student comes in thinking that glass cutting will be the most difficult skill to master. Many new students experience some level of anxiety during the early stages of the cutting instruction. But after the first two-hour session, most begin to feel a confidence in cutting that continues to grow.

This primer is intended to allay concerns you might have about cutting glass and get you ready to successfully cut your panel.

About Cutters

Many different glass cutters are on the market today, and most can be classified as either upright or pistol shaped. Choose a cutter that is comfortable to use and easy to maneuver. If you see yourself making numerous stained glass projects down the road, a cutter is one of three tools you should plan to spend some money on. Be advised that even though many budget-priced cutters are available, our experience has shown that they do not work as well and have a shorter life than the more expensive cutters. Plan to spend about 30 or 40 dollars for a quality cutter.

Holding the Cutter

Glass cutters should be held differently depending on the style that you select. The most common cutter is an upright steel or carbide wheel cutter with notches and a ball on top, so we will address that grip first.

1 Start by making a V with the first two fingers of your dominant hand, and slide the cutter between them. Place your index finger in the slot in the front and your thumb in the slot in the back. This hand position allows you to steady the cutter.

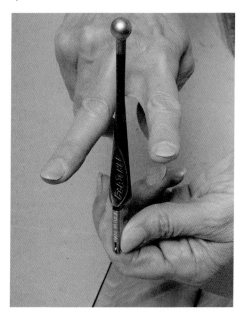

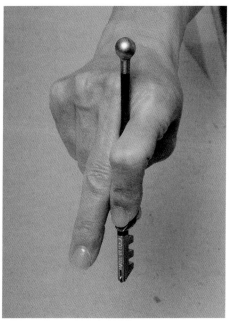

2 Place the thumb from your opposite hand on the ball or top of the cutter and your index finger along the side of the cutter as shown.

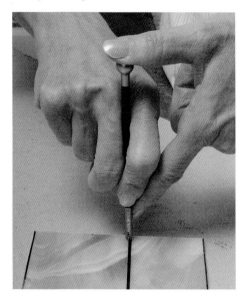

3 As you cut, create pressure on the glass by pushing down with your thumb on the ball; your index finger helps you guide the cutter. This cutter should be held perpendicular to the surface of the glass.

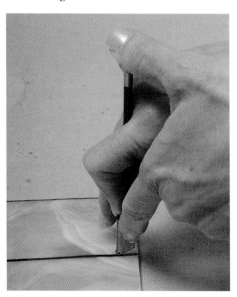

4 An effective grip for an upright pencil-shaped cutter is to hold it like a pencil in your dominant hand.

5 Now overlay this hand with your opposite hand, placing your index finger along the side of the cutter, just off the work surface. This cutter can be tilted back toward you as shown. Apply pressure from the three fingers holding the cylinder in order to score the glass.

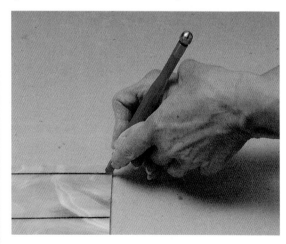

6 If you are using a pistol-shaped cutter, place it in your dominant hand with your thumb on top.

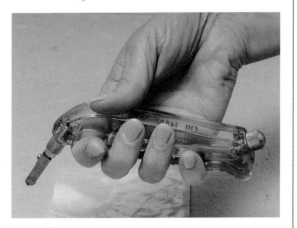

7 Now overlay your other hand on your dominant hand, moving your index finger along the side of the cutting wheel, just off the surface. The cutter handle should now be parallel to the glass surface with the cutting head angled back slightly.

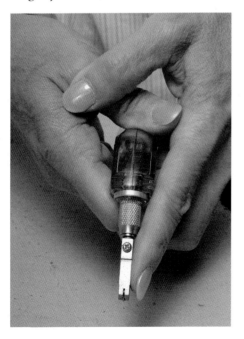

Feeling comfortable with your grip? Probably not, but stick with it—it will get better.

PRO TIP ✔

Cutting oil is used to lubricate the cutting wheel. This keeps the wheel turning freely and reduces friction between the wheel and the glass. For cutters without oil reservoirs, put a sponge in a baby food jar and saturate with oil. Dip your cutter in the oil every few times that you make a score. You can also store your cutter in the jar when it is not in use.

For self-oiling cutters, add oil to approximately 10% of capacity. Over-filling leads to leakage, and a little oil lasts a long time. Each day you use the cutter, open the oil reserve hole to allow air to enter. Failure to do this creates a vacuum, which may keep oil from feeding onto the wheel.

CAUTION: When replacing the screw, tighten lightly so as not to force the screw into the plastic handle, which could split the seam. This will cause significant and continual leakage.

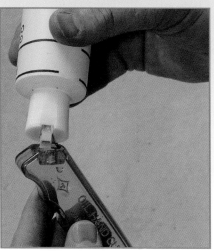

Cutting the Glass

When you begin your cutting practice, you should stand up. You will get better leverage on your cutter by using your large arm and shoulder muscles, and you will be able to see better if you are directly above your work.

When you align your cutter on a line marked on a piece of glass, you will notice a small slot at the bottom of the cutter; this is exactly where the cutting wheel is located. Starting now, and continuing through your entire stained glass career, train your eye to see this groove and line it up exactly with your pattern line during each and every cut. Now put on your safety glasses and let's do some cutting.

As you cut, you must put light pressure on the glass, which will make a slight gritting noise. This is referred to as "scoring." The result is a faint scratch on the glass. Once you have scored the glass, you will need to finish the break.

NOTE: Technically, you are not really cutting the glass with just your glass cutter. Rather it is a two-step process: 1) scoring, which means applying a slight scratch to the upper surface of the glass, and 2) breaking, which refers to separating glass along the score line using one of several techniques. For the sake of clarity, the term "cutting" will be used exclusively throughout the book to describe the two-step process.

1 On a sheet of glass approximately 4 inches by 6 inches (clear window glass is fine for practice cutting), use a marker to draw several lines across the glass. Holding your cutter as described, start your score $^1/16$ inch from the edge of the glass closest to you. You should be able to see the cutter's slot in the middle of the line during the entire score. Proceed to $^1/16$ inch from the opposite edge.

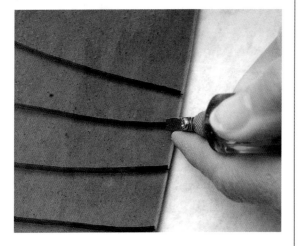

PRO TIPS ✔

1 For many new folks just starting out in the craft, there is a tendency to over-score, which results in a loud and scratchy noise. However, most people don't notice the noise because they are focusing on the process. This problem is easier to see than hear: If there is a heavy scratch with minute specks of crushed glass, the score is too hard. Lighten up.

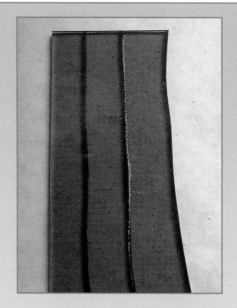

2 It is important to stop your cutter at the end of a score before it goes off the end. Failure to do this will frequently chip or crack the glass and will cause damage to the cutter over time.

Here is a good exercise to help you develop proper pressure on the glass:

Score a strip and then break with your running pliers. Now lighten your score on another strip and use the running pliers again. Repeat this until you only see a faint scratch from your cutter and your running pliers are still able to separate the glass.

3 Never go over a score line a second time. You will not get good results.

Breaking the Glass

You can choose one of three main ways to break the glass.

Manual break. Place your thumbs parallel to the score line about 1 inch apart. Your index fingers should be bent and curled under the glass as if you were about to snap a cracker in half. Now roll your thumbs outward with the same snapping motion. *Remember to always roll your thumbs outward.*

Using breaking pliers. If you score along a line that is about 1 inch or less from the edge of a piece of glass, the resulting strip will be too narrow to allow you to get the leverage to break it manually. You'll need to use breaking pliers. Notice that these pliers have a notched upper jaw and a curved lower jaw.

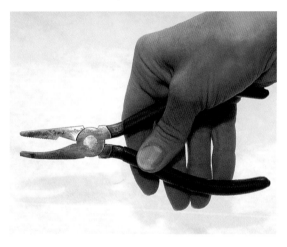

Grip the glass with these pliers perpendicular to the scored line, as shown. The pliers should be very close to the scored line but not on or over it.

Holding the pliers firmly, snap down using the same outward motion that you used for the manual break. The back of your hand will bend down. Do you see an equal amount of marker on both sides of your break?

Using running pliers. Running pliers allow for a more controlled break that starts at the beginning of a score and continues to the end. These pliers have two differently shaped jaws and a mark that indicates the top. They *must* be used with the top facing up. Reversing the grip can cause the glass to shatter.

Place the running pliers about ¹/₄ inch onto the glass, lining up the indicator mark with the scored line, as shown. Squeeze gently to separate the glass.

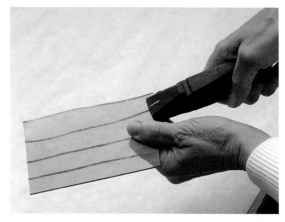

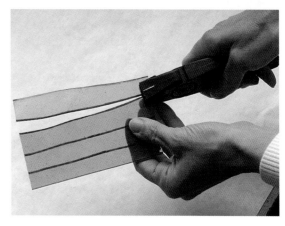

Now score several more strips and practice the three breaking techniques until you feel comfortable with them—you will use all three while working with stained glass.

PRO TIP ✔

1 To avoid chipping or scratching, never put your pliers on the actual piece you will be using.

2 Always break toward a point to prevent it from breaking off.

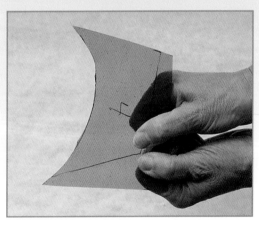

Cutting Shapes With Straight Edges

On pieces of scrap glass about 4 inches by 5 inches, draw the practice pieces (see page 25).

To cut out practice piece 1 start on the edge of the glass closest to you, about $^1/16$ inch from the edge (this shape can be cut in any order).

Score across the glass to the opposite side. Remember to stop $^1/16$ inch from the edge.

Pattern Pieces for Cutting Practice

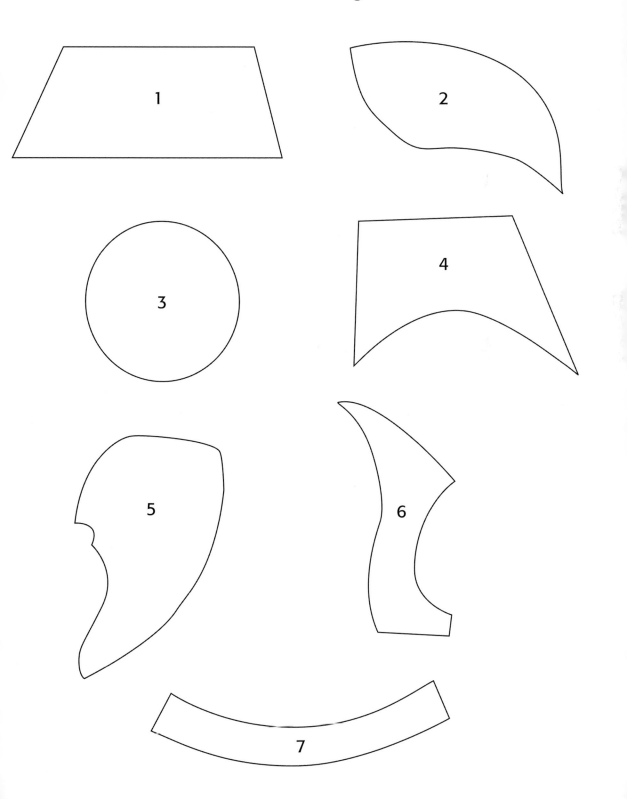

Break off the glass at the score line using any of the three breaking techniques.

Now score and break the three remaining sides, one at a time. Score down the center of your mark so you can see how you are doing. The scrap you break off and the finished piece should have equal amounts of marker along the edges.

Cutting Inside and Outside Curves

Practice piece 2 has both inside and outside curves. You should always cut the inside curves first. You will do this in three stages, as indicated by the three small arcs.

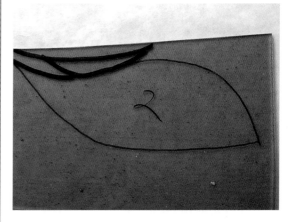

Begin by cutting the outermost arc.

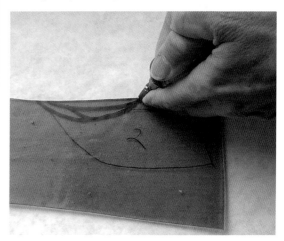

Cut the next arc.

Cut the remaining section in the curve.

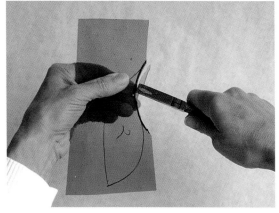

Cut a portion of the outside curve as shown. Then cut the remaining part of the curve.

Cut a portion of the remaining curve as shown.

To cut out the circle, start at the top right. Cut the first segment.

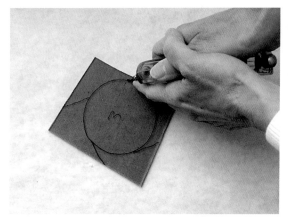

Finish cutting the rest of the outside curve.

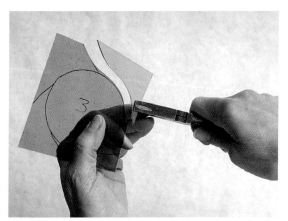

Piece 3 is a circle that's cut out in a series of outside curves (five are shown here).

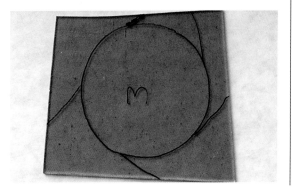

Cut the remaining arcs, one at a time.

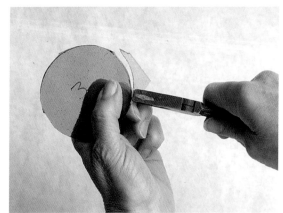

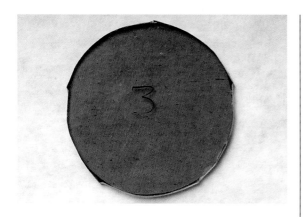

Piece 4 represents the most difficult piece of glass to cut: a deep inside curve. If you were to score the entire inside curve and proceed to break it out, it would likely break off near one or both points. To avoid this, you must remove the glass in segments.

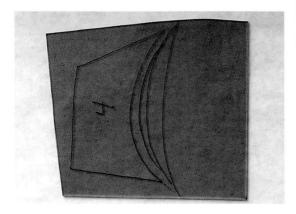

First, score along the outermost segment and break off the excess glass.

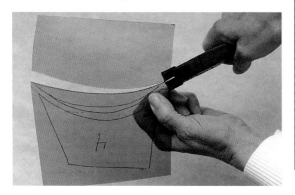

Now, as you work your way into the actual pattern line, you must be more cautious. Score along the next arc.

Instead of pulling *down* with your breaking pliers, place your pliers on one end of the score and pull *back and down* at the same time. You should hear a little click and see a separation run from your pliers to about midway along the score.

Place your pliers on the opposite end of the score and, again, pull them back and down. You will hear another click as the new run will meet the end of the first run. The glass will completely separate.

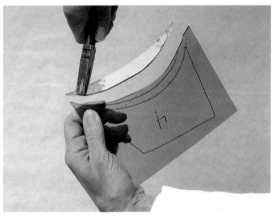

Cut out the next arc.

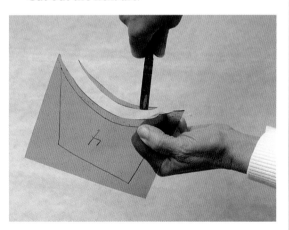

You should have pared the glass to about $^1/4$ inch along the curve.

Cut about a third of the remaining curve. It's helpful to make dotted lines to indicate the starting and stopping points.

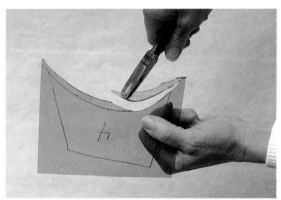

Cut another third of the curve from the opposite end.

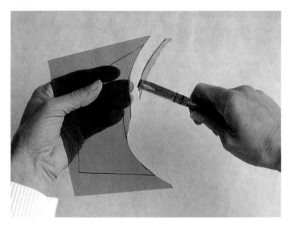

Score and break the remaining arc.

PRO TIP ✔

When you encounter a deep inside curve:

1 Be sure to have excess glass in back of the curve, and

2 Cut the inside curve first.

3 If you have back-to-back inside curves, like in the practice piece from the tulip design, cut the deeper curve first.

Now score one of the sides. Hold your pliers at the top of the piece and break toward one of the points.

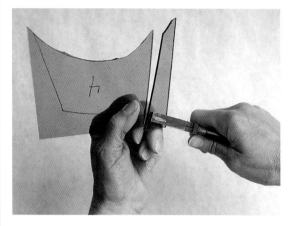

Finish cutting the two remaining sides.

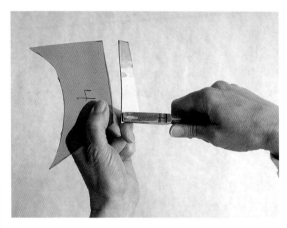

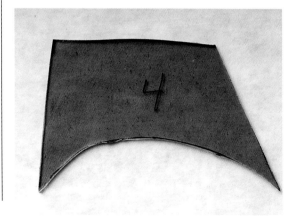

Pieces 5, 6, and 7 are from the featured panel design, and the cutting processes for these pieces are detailed toward the beginning of chapter 7. Look ahead to this section and try cutting these shapes from some practice glass.

Continue cutting the practice pieces or other shapes from the panel pattern until you are feeling comfortable with the results.

PRO TIP ✔

The three methods discussed for breaking glass can be interchanged for many breaks. The rule of thumb is that you use a manual break when possible simply to avoid picking up a tool and wasting time. However, if you develop a preference for one technique, by all means use it.

There will be many times when one method will work better than others. If you are initially squeamish about manual breaking, force yourself to do it. Start with 1- to 2-inch-long strips, and work up to longer scores.

Get to know and feel comfortable with your breaking pliers. They will become your friend.

Grozing

Grozing is the process by which tiny bits of glass are removed from a larger piece of glass. Grozing is employed if, after you have cut out a glass shape, small amounts of scrap still remain.

To practice grozing, take a piece of glass and draw an arc 1 inch wide and about $1/8$ inch deep.

Turn your grozing pliers over so the curved jaw is on top. Hold the pliers at about a 45-degree angle to the glass and about $1/16$ inch onto the glass, as shown.

Take a firm but not crushing hold on the glass and twist the pliers back and down. Remember, you are not trying to crush through the glass—you are just pulling small pieces loose.

Proceed along the area you are removing, taking only a small amount with each twist.

To clean out the last small bits of glass, turn the pliers 90 degrees to the glass. Take hold of the glass bits and rotate your pliers down to pull off the glass nubs. You will probably have to do this several times at each place in order to make it fairly smooth.

Achieving proficiency at grozing requires practice; work on it a while.

PRO TIP ✔

Often, particularly in the early stages of your glass cutting career, you will be faced with the pieces that, after they have been cut, still have excess glass that extends beyond the pattern. Generally, excess glass of 1/16 inch or more can and should be removed by scoring and breaking. The glass will not break off cleanly and you will still need to do some grozing.

Smoothing and Grinding

The final shaping of the glass is done with either a carborundum stone or an electric grinder.

If you are using a stone, wet it with water for about 10 seconds so the glass will stay cool as it's ground. Firmly move the stone back and forth along the edge of the glass. Never move the stone perpendicular to the glass; that angle will cause the glass to chip.

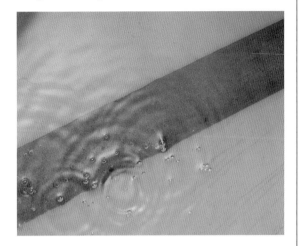

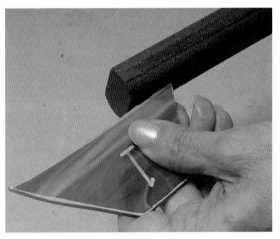

Or you can move the glass along a stationary stone to achieve the same result.

The preferred method for smoothing glass is to use an electric grinder. This specialty tool employs a water-cooled diamond grinding drum. Glass grinders are safe, fast, and very effective.

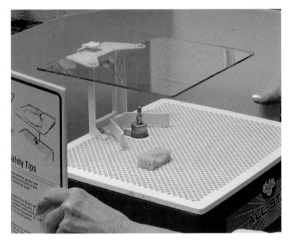

The sponge behind the grinder wheel is soaked in water to keep the glass cool as grinding occurs. Lay the glass flat on the surface. Push the glass against the wheel with a slight pressure, grinding right up to the pattern edge. A perfectly ground piece is one that shows no glass protruding beyond the paper pattern.

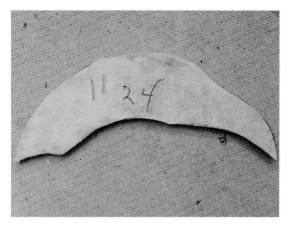

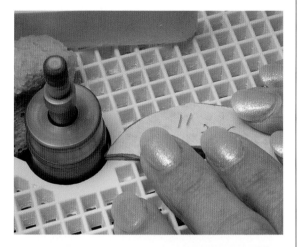

PRO TIP ✔

Push the glass in one direction; avoid a back-and-forth sanding motion. If you notice a buildup of dry powder when you are grinding, clean your sponge and make sure it is making contact with the grinding bit, or add a little water. If a lot of water is appearing on the pattern piece, dump a little out.

4

Cutting and Soldering Lead

OVER THE YEARS, COUNTLESS STUDENTS HAVE asked us which method is harder, copper foil or lead? Our response is that neither is necessarily harder than the other. They are just different.

Working with lead came requires several skills that are different from those required when working with copper foil; they include accurate lead cutting and proper soldering of joints. This chapter is intended to give you detailed information about how to build a small leaded panel in order to teach you techniques you will use in creating the large panel in chapter 8.

Cutting Lead

Lead came, or channel, is available in two styles: U-lead and H-lead.

The U and H designations refer to the profiles of each. U-lead has a single channel and is typically used as an outside border.

H-lead has two channels and is generally used within a project, allowing pieces of glass to be connected. Both lead types come in many sizes, depending on the application. The leads used in the small panel "Sunrise from the Cove" are $1/4$-inch U on the outside and $3/16$-inch H in the interior. The illustration below shows the terms associated with the parts of the U and H cames. Lead size is measured along the face of the came. The $3/16$-inch H-lead was chosen because of the small size of the panel—10 inches in diameter. If the panel were twice this size, $1/4$-inch H-lead would probably be more suitable.

There are two main tools for cutting lead cames: a lead knife and lead cutters, or dykes.

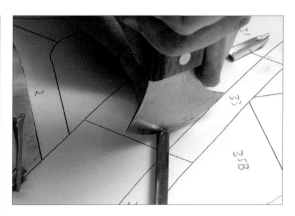

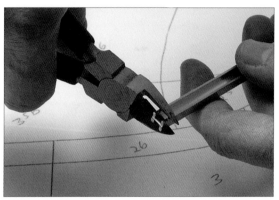

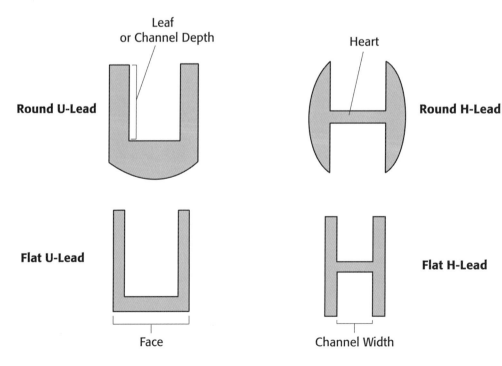

Round U-Lead

Leaf
or Channel Depth

Flat U-Lead

Face

Round H-Lead

Heart

Flat H-Lead

Channel Width

Lead dykes will likely be your tool of choice since they are easier to use. But they have their limitations—they can cut only a limited angle. Dykes work well for 90-degree cuts and slight angles, but more severe angles require a knife. The photo below shows just about the maximum angle that dykes can cut properly.

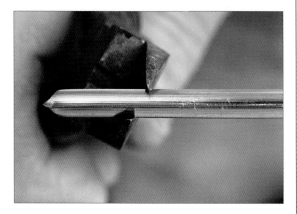

When cutting with the dykes, you must be aware of two things: 1) The flanges of the came must face you. 2) The flat side of the dykes must face the piece of lead that you will be using (the concave side will face the trimmed scrap piece).

Here the dykes are cutting across both flanges, with the flat side facing the piece of lead we want to use in the project.

The side of the lead that was in the concave side of the dykes gets crimped and is unusable (the crimped edge must be trimmed off before you measure off another piece of lead).

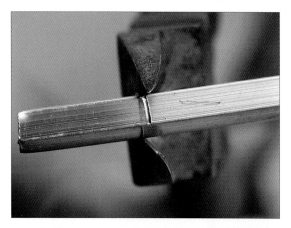

Cutting against the sides of the came results in crushing and makes the lead unusable.

To cut a proper angle with dykes, three conditions must be met: 1) The top blade of the dykes must be on top of the scratch mark (which you make with a horseshoe nail to indicate where to cut). 2) The bottom blade must be on the bottom of the scratch mark. 3) The top blade must be perpendicular to the lead.

Here the first two conditions are met. But the top blade is not perpendicular to the lead. This is wrong.

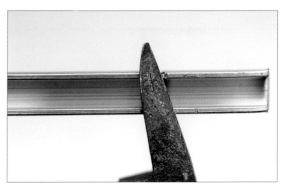

To practice cutting lead, make scratch marks on scrap pieces indicating various angles to be cut, and then trim them off. Remember to keep the top blade on the top of the mark, the bottom blade on the bottom of the mark, and the top blade perpendicular to the lead.

A good, sharp lead knife can be used to cut lead at a variety of angles and is an indispensable tool. Besides cutting lead, it is also useful for lifting glass into lead channels, bending flanges of cut lead that get bent, pushing leads into place, and so on.

To cut with a lead knife, lay the came flat on its face.

Set the knife on your scratch mark and rock it back and forth several times while pressing down on the lead.

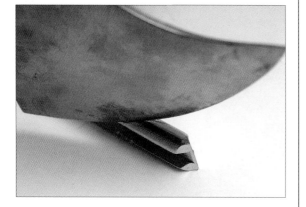

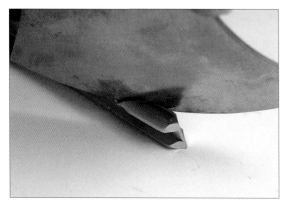

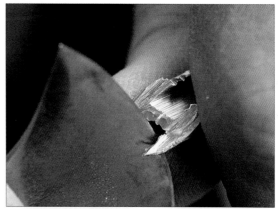

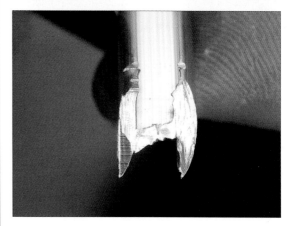

If a leaf of the came folds a bit, bend it back with the knife.

You have to apply moderate pressure on the lead in order to cut through it, and you usually need to rock back and forth five to ten times to make a complete cut.

Getting the Pattern Ready

Chapter 7 gives detailed instructions on how to prepare a pattern for the large panel. The process of setting up for this small panel is the same. In general, you must make two additional copies of the pattern. Using tracing paper and carbon paper, trace the pattern onto a sheet of oak tag. Number the pieces, color-code, and include directional lines for grain direction.

Cut the pattern apart using pattern shears for lead.

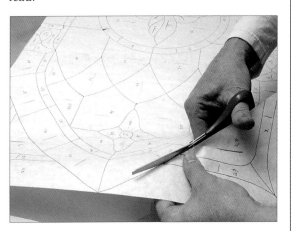

Attach the pattern pieces to your glass with rubber cement.

Cut out and grind your glass.

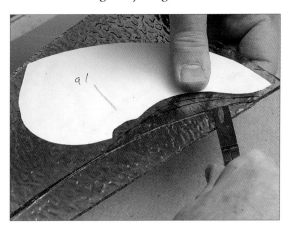

Leading the Glass

1 To lead the glass for the small panel, cut out ten pieces each of the U and H cames, making each about $1/2$ inch long. These will be used to temporarily secure glass pieces and as spacers. We will refer to them as "scrap leads." Starting at the bottom of the pattern, secure a piece of the outside border glass by placing two U-shaped scrap leads on the outside and securing them with horseshoe nails. Then, place an H-shaped scrap lead over the inside of the glass piece, directly on the pattern line.

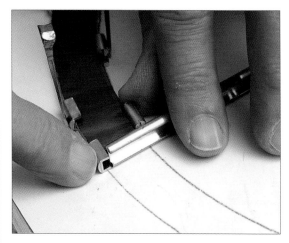

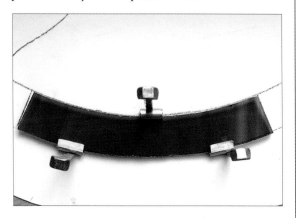

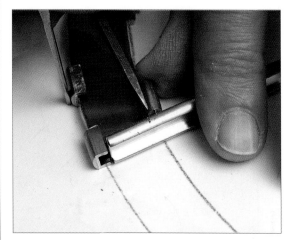

2 Hold another U scrap lead over the outside of the glass. Push a strip of H scrap lead against it, as shown. Put an H scrap lead spacer over the inside of the glass up against the longer H lead strip. Scratch the lead strip with a nail where it needs to be cut in order to fit between the two lead scrap pieces.

3 Cut the lead and repeat this process until you have the bottom four border pieces joined and secured.

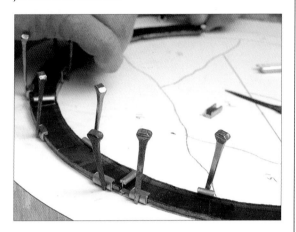

PRO TIPS ✔

• Horseshoe nails should be driven so that the flat side of the nail goes against the lead. This avoids gouging or marring of the lead.

• Drive each nail straight rather than at an angle.

• Every time you get a lead piece fitted, hold it in place with a nail as well.

• Be sure to drive the nails with enough force to secure the glass or lead.

• When removing a nail, wiggle it back and forth a few times and lift out.

4 Take a strip of the H lead at least 2 feet long. Bend it into a curve that approximates the inside curve of the four pieces of border glass.

7 Cut the lead at the mark.

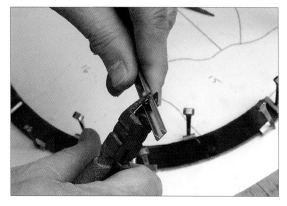

5 Push it down against the nails holding the glass pieces in place. Be sure to have at least 1 inch of lead extending out from both ends.

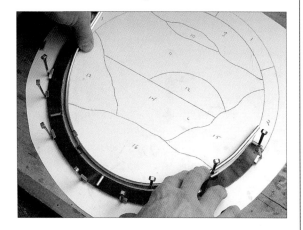

8 Remove the first two nails and lead scraps on the inner circle. Fit the end of the lead strip over the glass and secure it with a nail.

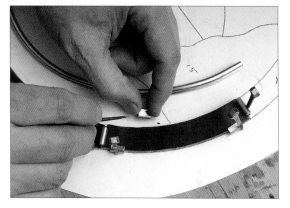

6 Scratch a mark on one end of lead, opposite the small lead at the end of the glass.

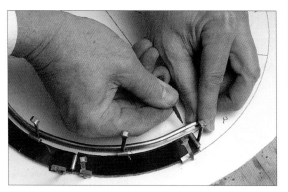

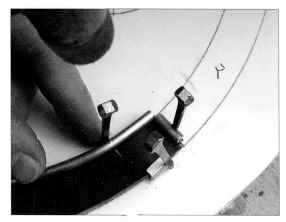

9 Continue pushing the lead strip over the glass, securing it with nails about every 6 inches.

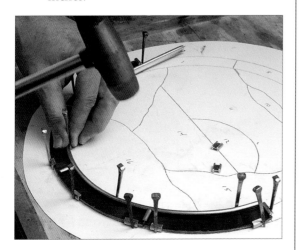

10 As you come to the end, scratch the lead strip where it meets the center of the small lead piece holding the last piece of border glass in.

11 Pull the lead away from the glass about 1 inch; turn your dykes perpendicular to the lead, with the flat side facing the end you are using. Cut it cleanly.

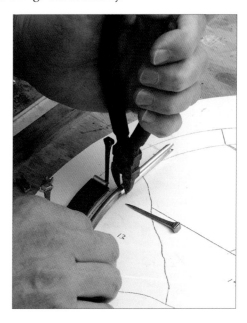

12 Push the lead back over the glass edge and secure it with a nail.

13 Take piece number 16 (the bottom water) and bend a piece of H-lead along its upper edge. Overlap the lead at the beginning of the piece of glass.

14 Because piece number 16 will fit into the lead you fitted over the four border pieces, the lead that goes over the upper edge will need to be cut short on both sides. Set an H-lead scrap on the side edge of the glass to determine where to cut the larger lead. Scratch a mark that is an extension of the line coming up from the scrap lead.

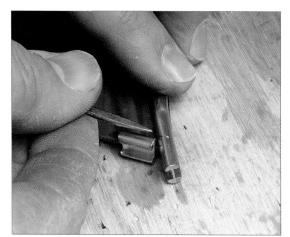

15 Cut the angle.

16 Hold the lead in place and bend it along the contours of the glass.

17 At the end, use a scrap lead to determine the angle for cutting the second end.

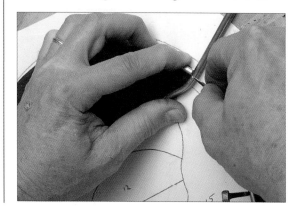

18 Cut the lead.

19 Remove only enough nails to allow the lower water piece to be inserted into the lead. Tap the glass lightly with the lead hammer until it is fully seated into the lead. You should see the pattern line.

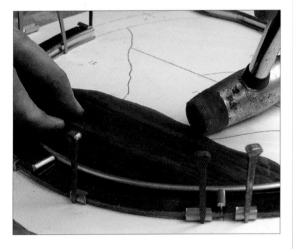

20 Take the lead strip you just cut out and set it along the water piece. It is often helpful to raise the glass slightly with a lead knife, making it easier to fit the lead over the glass. Hold the lead in place with two nails on opposite ends.

21 Take the left rock formation piece (number 13) and cut a piece of lead for the right side of it using the same method you did with the top of the water lead. Hold in place with two nails.

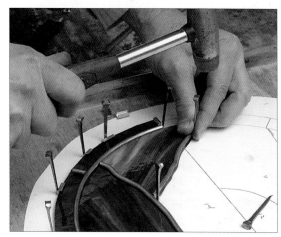

22 Install the right rock formation piece (number 15) in the same way.

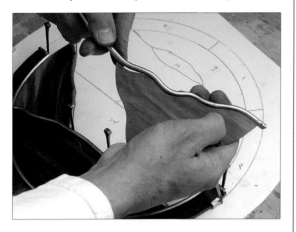

23 Install the upper water piece (number 14).

24 Lay a piece of lead over one of the side leads and scratch the appropriate angle. This angle is too severe for the lead dykes—you will need your lead knife here. Rock the knife back and forth while pushing down with moderate pressure. Be sure to keep the knife blade perpendicular to the surface.

It is easy to misjudge the exact angle; this one does not fit well.

If this happens, remeasure and cut the lead again with the knife—or take off small pieces from both the top and bottom faces with the lead dykes.

25 Cut the opposite end of the lead and fit it over the glass. Hold in place with a nail.

26 Cut a piece of lead to go around the curved edge of the sun. Cut both ends short so the lead meets the side leads.

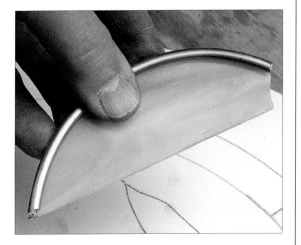

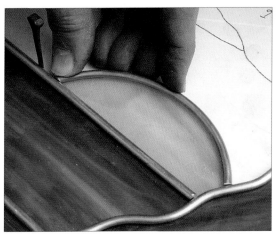

27 Install the large sky piece (number 11) and hold it in place with nails on both sides.

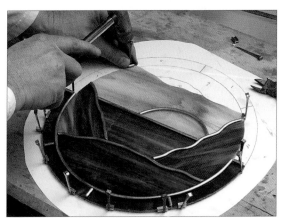

28 Cut the correct angle on the left of the lead piece.

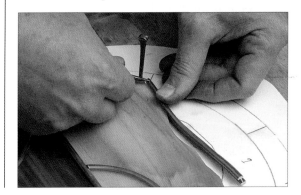

29 Bend it along the glass, past where the cloud piece ends. This lead will be mitered (cut at an angle) to fit against another lead that will fit over the cloud and along the right end of the large sky piece.

Use a scrap H-lead to determine the angle that needs to be cut.

30 Set the cloud piece in position. On both ends, miter the lead piece that fits over the cloud and continues to the edge of the large sky piece. Both of these miters will need to be fashioned with the lead knife. These are challenging, so attempt to make them flush with their adjoining leads.

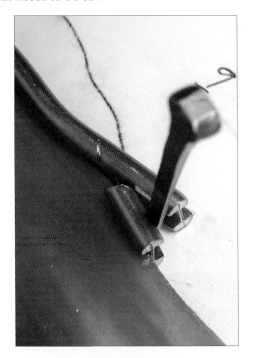

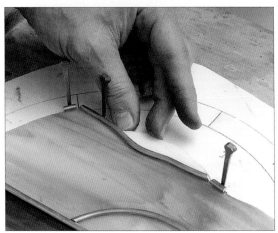

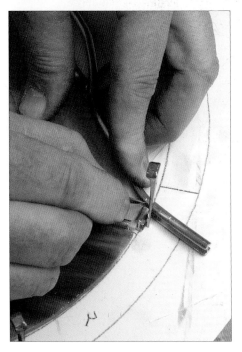

31 Install the top sky piece.

32 Starting on the left side, place one end of a two-foot piece of lead on the outside edges of the glass pieces you just installed. Be sure to butt it up against the lead that was previously installed inside the four border pieces of glass. Bend it around the sky pieces, cutting it where it meets the lead on the opposite side.

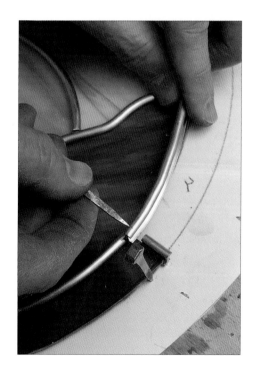

33 Insert the remaining four border pieces with connecting short leads between them.

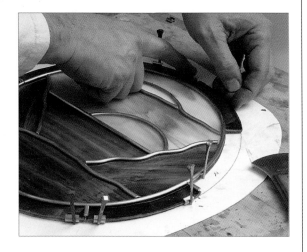

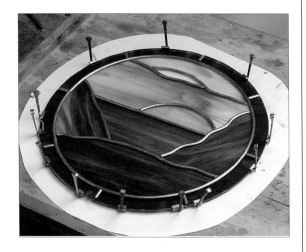

34 You will need at least 3 feet of U-lead for the outside of the panel. Start in the middle of one short connecting lead. Place the U-lead over the glass and hold it in place with a nail.

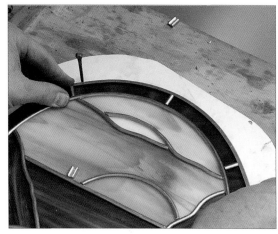

35 Continue bending the lead around the panel, inserting nails as you go to hold the glass tight.

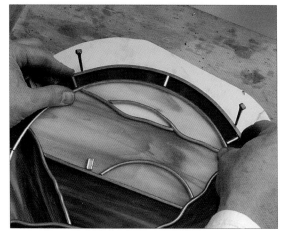

36 Miter the lead at the end so that it is flush with the lead where you started.

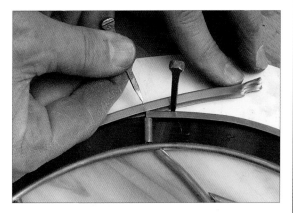

37 Hold it with a nail.

Soldering the Panel

Plug in your soldering iron. When working with lead, you want a cooler iron than when working with copper foil. If you have a Temptrol iron from Inland, set the dial so the arrow points straight up. For other irons, solder should melt immediately when it touches the iron tip, and you should be able to hold the iron on the lead for a second or two without the lead melting. Test the heat a few times on scrap pieces of lead before you start soldering your panel.

1 Be sure the flux is not dripping off the brush. Make one brushstroke at each lead joint. About two full brushes of flux will be sufficient for each side of the panel.

2 You will be melting off about $^1/_8$ inch of the solder at each point. Unwind about 6 inches of solder and place the end on a lead intersection. Bring the iron down onto the solder, melting it and allowing it to flow evenly at the lead joint. Lift the solder out of the way. Hold the iron down for a count of "one thousand one" and lift it up slowly, avoiding a shaking motion.

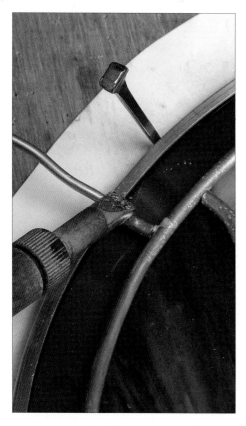

The solder joints should be in the shape of a T.

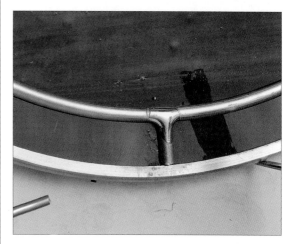

PRO TIP ✔

If you are getting large lumps of solder, apply a little flux, re-melt the solder and pull some of the excess onto the glass. It will cool quickly and you can then remove it from the glass.

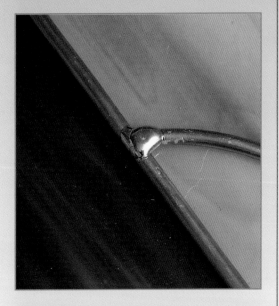

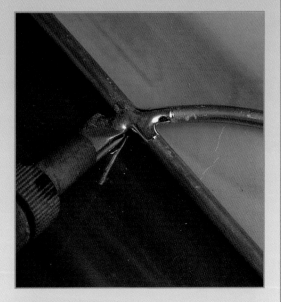

3 Complete the soldering on the front side, remove the nails, and turn the panel over.

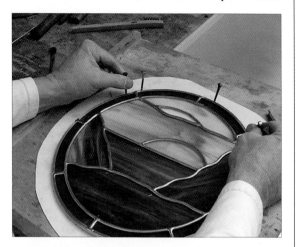

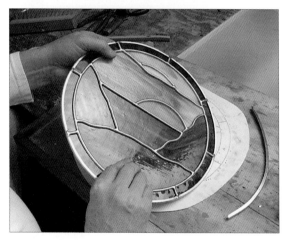

Be sure to apply flux to the second side. It is very easy to miss fluxing a joint or two. Without flux, the solder goes on in a blob. If this happens, put a little flux on the blob and melt it flat.

It is also quite common, particularly on the back, to have a lead joint where the leads are not quite flush. If this happens, cut a scrap piece of lead up the heart and bend it up with the dykes.

Mark and cut a small cross-section of lead and insert it as a filler. Push it into the open space and make it fit tightly.

Flux and solder the joint.

4 Finish all the soldering.

A Few More Tips

Can you tell which of these joints is formed correctly? Number 2 is correct. The two long leads each have two different angle cuts. On the side facing the glass, the leads are mitered by snipping off segments of the upper and lower leaves. The marker line shown on the glass is a guide for the proper angle. The angle on the opposite side of the same joint is also formed by snipping top and bottom sections of the leaves. These are cut at a slightly different angle. This allows the small lead piece (cut at the same angle) to fit flush against the two larger leads. This is referred to as an arrow cut.

Notice how the other three corners of the diamond don't fit as well as number 2.

The teardrop jewel (number 5) has its lead mitered at its points. To accomplish this, snip lead leaves top and bottom. Because the inside angle is so acute, the outside leaves can be cut to form a flat shelf to accept a piece of connecting lead that is cut straight across.

At intersections 6 and 7, notice the different angles of the miters. At intersection 9, the three leads are all arrow cuts. Intersection 8 does not fit properly.

Notice the proper mitering for the corners of a square. At intersection 10, the small lead that meets the squared corner has an arrow that fits into the other two leads.

The circular jewel gets wrapped with continuous lead. The miter is always placed where another lead meets the circle.

The three-piece cluster with the red jewel is identical to the ones featured in the lead panel. The lead starts at the top right side of the jewel, and bends around the jewel. Set it against the left white piece and continue bending it around the top of the same white piece. A small lead is then mitered against the larger lead and again at the straight border leads.

The examples in these photos illustrate many of the configurations you will be faced with when mitering leads in the featured panel. It might be helpful to refer to these illustrations as you work.

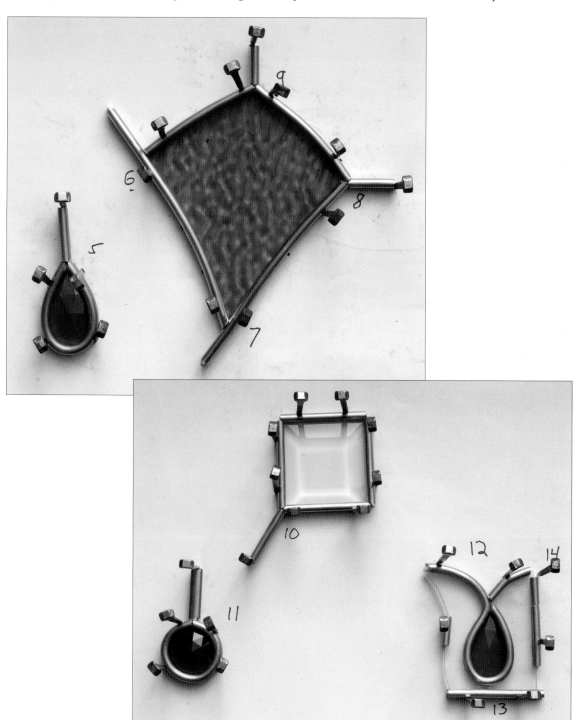

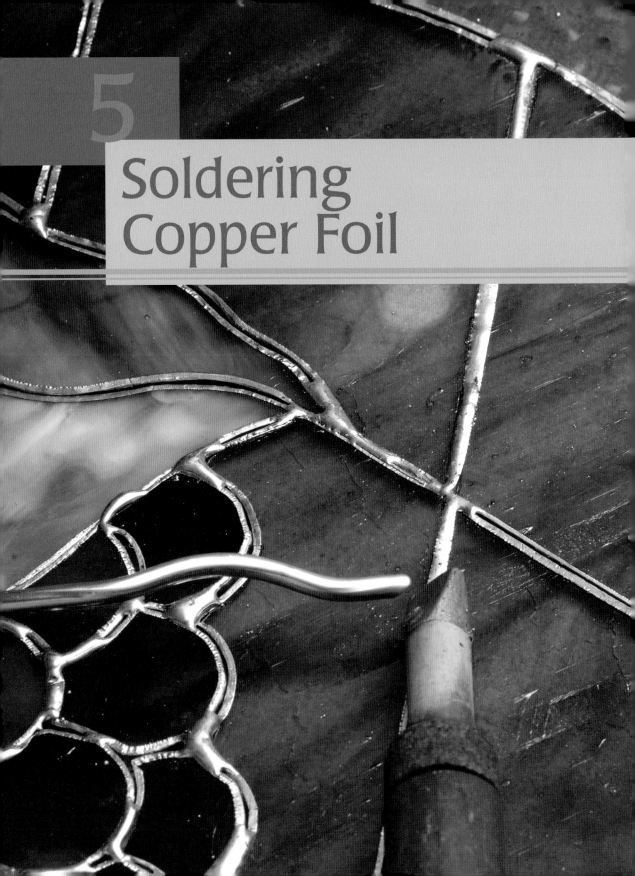

5

Soldering
Copper Foil

NEARLY ALL OUR NEW STUDENTS THINK THAT cutting glass will be the most difficult part of the stained glass process. However, after about an hour or so of cutting practice, most people realize it's not too bad.

Soldering, though, is a different story. The majority of new students struggle to different degrees with achieving consistently smooth solder seams. With practice, this will eventually come, but it does take some time.

If you have not done much soldering, or any at all, I recommend that you practice by completing one of the circular inset panels from the pattern section. This will give you lots of good experience. It could also be a nice addition to a small powder room or a gift to someone special for the holidays. Build it with or without the circular glass border. So choose whichever design you want.

Soldering the Panel

Chapter 7 gives details on the early steps of making this panel, from pattern development through applying copper foil. The steps are, for the most part, the same as those for the small leaded panel project, except that foil shears are used to cut apart the pattern and, of course, the edges of the glass pieces are wrapped with copper foil.

1 After you've laid out the foiled glass on the oak tag sheet and used pushpins around the circle to secure the glass in place, apply flux to all the solder seams. Don't worry about putting flux on the outside of the circle.

About two brushfuls of flux will be sufficient for each side of the project. To avoid using too much, brush off the excess in your flux jar before you start.

2 After applying flux, realign any glass pieces that might have shifted in the process.

3 Plug in your soldering iron; most take about five minutes to heat up. While it does, you can saturate a sponge with water and place it in the tray on the iron stand.

It's important to have your iron set at a proper temperature. If you are using a temperature-controlled iron, or one with a reostatic control, you will need to do a test. Touch a small amount of solder to your iron. If it melts instantly and does not fall off, the temperature is about right. If it doesn't melt right away, turn up the temperature; if the solder falls off right away, turn the temperature down.

4 Hold the iron in your dominant hand and the spool of solder in the other.

PRO TIP ✔

When you first heat up your iron, it is a good idea to clean the tip. The iron is subjected to very high temperatures (more than 700 degrees Fahrenheit) and ash frequently gets baked onto the tip. This impedes the transfer of heat, preventing the solder from melting.

Sal ammoniac is a chemical block (looks like a bar of soap) that loosens ash. To use it, dig out a small trough on the block and melt a small amount of solder in it. Rub both sides of the tip back and forth several times in the molten solder. Clean the tip in the sponge and resume soldering.

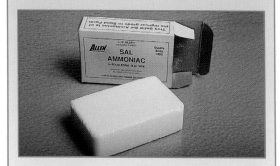

When you solder for an extended time, you might sense the iron cooling down. It probably just needs to be cleaned in sal ammoniac.

5 Unwind about 6 inches of solder from the spool. Set the end on an intersection where three or more pieces of glass touch. Place the iron on the solder and melt off about $1/8$ inch. This is referred to as tack soldering.

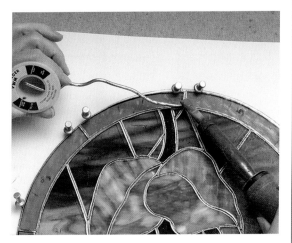

Don't worry if the solder is a little flat or high. The amount of solder is not important at this point. The objective is simply to connect all of the pieces.

6 Lift the solder out of the way first, then lift the iron.

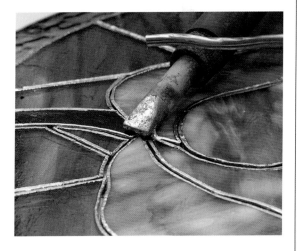

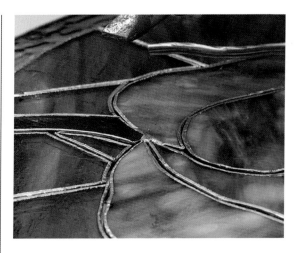

7 Finish tack soldering all pieces in the panel and remove the pins.

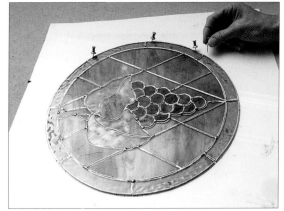

8 Now you'll apply the first coat of solder. Start at the top of the panel. Hold your iron like you are holding a sword or shaking hands. The barrel of the iron should be parallel to the surface of the glass.

9 Tilt the iron so the tip is at a 45-degree angle to the foiled seam. The iron can rest right on the seam.

10 Find a hot spot on the iron (a spot where the solder melts instantly). This is generally toward the back of the iron.

11 Push the solder to the iron and, as it melts, pull the iron and solder toward you. Working toward yourself allows you to see the area that is being soldered and adjust the amount of solder being applied. Do not worry about how the solder looks at this stage. The objective is to apply a relativity flat coating of solder to the entire panel.

12 Finish flat soldering the front side of the panel.

PRO TIP ✔

From time to time, you will notice gray ash forming on the iron tip. Remove this frequently by rubbing the iron on the wet sponge once on each side.

13 Next, you'll apply the second coat, or bead coat, of solder on top of the flat coat. The bead coat is a slightly rounded mound of solder. It should be of a consistent height throughout the panel, and it should be smooth. Sounds simple, but you will have to work at it to get good results.

Hold the iron in the same handshake manner. And again, start on a seam at the top of the panel and work toward you. To raise the height of the solder seam, add additional solder and pull the iron toward you as it melts.

14 Be careful not to add too much solder. If you find the solder building up, or forming blobs, pull it to an area that can use additional solder or pull it off the panel. To do this, melt the blob and drag it where you want it to go.

15 As you work around a cluster of small pieces, such as the grapes, turn your iron so that just one corner of the tip makes contact with the solder. It is easier to smooth out solder this way.

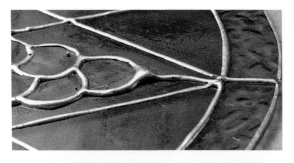

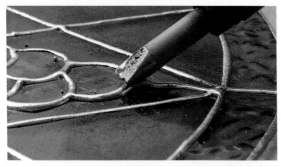

16 Continue beading the front side. When you are finished, check for high, low, or rough spots by running your finger along all solder seams.

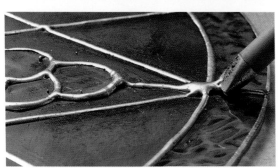

17 Turn the panel over and flux all the seams.

Notice that the solder has filled all the spaces and some has come through from the front side. This will make it easier to apply a bead coat on the first pass.

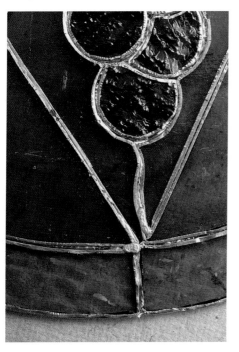

18 Apply a bead coat to all copper seams. Again, if you have areas where the solder is too heavy, melt the excess and pull it into an area where there is not enough solder, or drag it off.

19 When you are happy with the soldering on the back side, turn the panel over for a quick check on side one. Frequently, you will find an area that has melted back through. If so, flux the area, melt the solder, and spread it around the adjacent seams.

If you had several areas that melted through to the front side, you are either working too slowly or the iron is too hot.

PRO TIPS ✔

A few tricks you can employ when soldering:

- When holes or pits form while soldering, place the tip of your iron on the affected area, keep it in place for one second, then slowly lift up.

- If you're getting some spritzing from the flux while you solder, try wiping off some of the flux with an old cloth.

- If solder forms into a blob or spreads onto the glass, apply a little flux and then remelt the solder, pulling it along the seam.

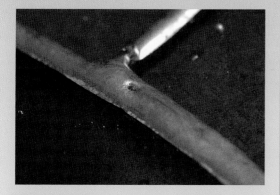

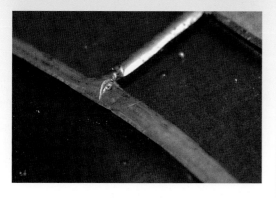

- When solder cools, it begins to oxidize and this interferes with remelting it. Apply a little flux first and the solder should flow nicely.

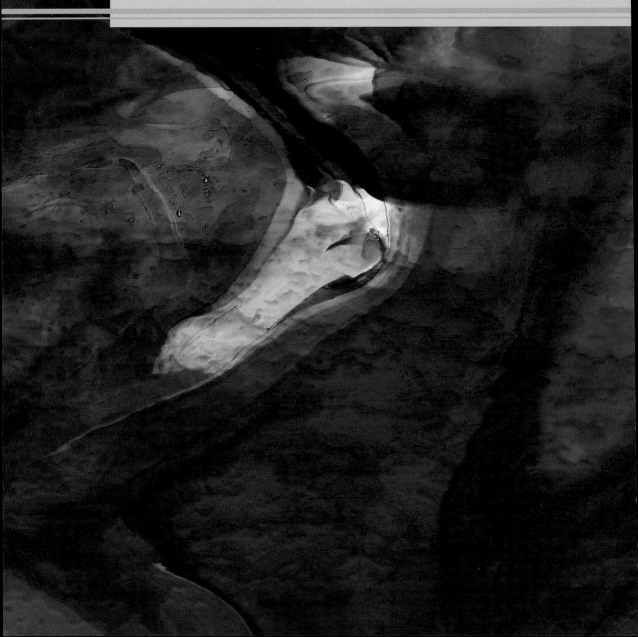

6

Selecting Your Glass

THE SINGLE MOST IMPORTANT STEP IN THE entire construction of a panel is the selection of your glass. Tightly fitting seams, smooth solder lines, an even patina, and a classy frame will all be overlooked if the glass you use does not work. This is also an opportunity for you, as the artist, to express yourself. Think of your glass collection as a color palette. Each time you procure new glass, your options will increase. Soon, instead of thinking green, you will be thinking about different shades of green, or blends that might include blues, browns, and reds. Stained glass is a colorful art with many, many colors available.

If you have limited experience in color coordination, a good learning exercise is to study stained glass design books and note what appeals to you and what doesn't. The authors are often professional designers and will offer examples of glass colors and styles that go nicely together. Once you have studied others' works, you will be in a better position to express your own vision.

Another way to learn about glass selection is to visit historic buildings, churches, and museums or simply take a stroll through the older sections of cities or towns. You might find this very enlightening. Having a camera handy will help you develop a permanent reference.

About Glass

Most stained glass can be separated into three main categories: cathedral, streaky, and opalescent.

Cathedral

Streaky

Opalescent

Cathedral glasses are single colored and available in a host of textures, including water, seedy, ripple, hammered, granite, and glue chip.

Water Glass

Hammered

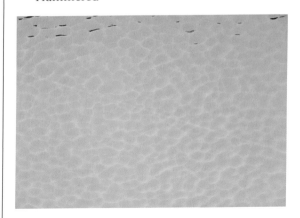

Granite

Glue Chip

Cathedrals are transparent; however, different textures will affect the degree of transparency. Using a seedy glass in a window panel will maximize visibility through the panel. The same window made of ripple glass offers a greater degree of privacy.

Seedy Glass

Ripple Glass

Streaky glasses are cathedrals with streaks of one or more cathedral colors. They may be smooth or textured, such as ripple, granite, or hammered.

Hammered Streaky

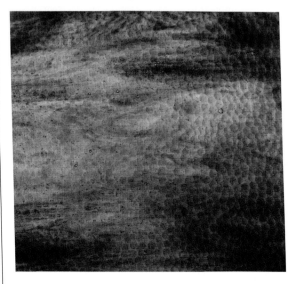

Granite Streaky

Two-color Mixed Streaky

Opalescent glasses ("opals" for short) are made up of varying amounts of white (opal) glass mixed with colored glass. The higher the opal content, the denser the glass will be. Some opals are single-colored, but most are multi-colored.

Opals have different degrees of density.

Low

Medium

High

A new innovative surface available from Spectrum Glass is their Corsica texture; it's found in their line of "Pearl Opal" glasses.

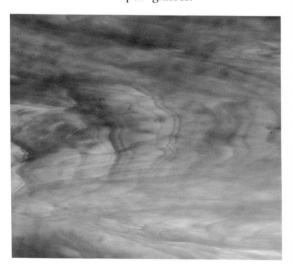

Other Specialty Glasses

Iridized glass has a shiny, mother-of-pearl coating on one side.

Art glass is usually hand-rolled in the old tradition.

Youghiogheny Stipple

Oceana Mottled

Van Gogh Glass is clear glue chip that has been painted on the back. This glass is almost totally opaque and has a wonderful, almost-three-dimensional reflective quality.

Uroboros Multicolored

Reamy Baroque by Spectrum

Bevels are precut pieces of glass with angled edges that create a prism or rainbow effect when sunlight passes through them. They are available in a multitude of shapes.

Jewels are faceted or smooth pieces of glass used as decorative features in stained glass projects. They are available in many colors. Jewels are used in our featured panel.

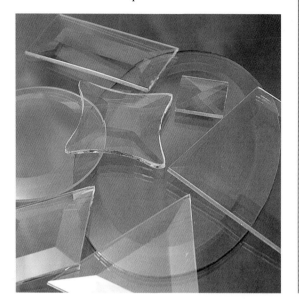

The following glass selections were used in the two featured panels:

Component	Quantity Needed	Lead Panel	Foil Panel
Outside Border	$2^1/2$ to 3 feet	K140	S4221W
Inside Border	$1^1/2$ to 2 feet	K266	S5331W
Star	$^3/4$ foot	K162MLG	W1455P
Border Pedestals	1 foot	W58	S1108W
Lower Background	$2^1/2$ feet	W01S	S100A
Circle Background	1 foot	W58LLG	5911W
Upper Background	1 foot	W257D	K28L
Kites	$^3/4$ foot	W238	EM4907
Circle Border	1 foot	W01S	S53331W
Flame	$^1/2$ foot	W11LL	xx
Tulips	$^1/2$ foot	xx	W2LL
Leaves	$^1/2$ foot	xx	W101LL

S—Spectrum, K—Kokomo, W—Wissmach, EM—English Muffle (Wissmach).

7

Preparing the Large Panel Project

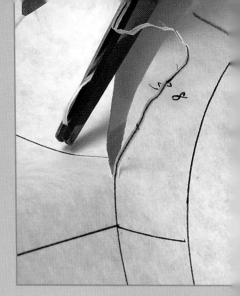

WHETHER YOU'VE DECIDED TO MAKE A PANEL using lead came or copper foil, the initial steps will be the same. This chapter begins with pattern setup and ends with glass cutting. Chapters 8 and 9 will detail the process for completing the panel using either method.

The pattern acts as a guide and blueprint for your project through the soldering stage. It dictates the shape of each piece of glass, and where the piece gets placed on your workboard. It helps you keep the project the intended size and shape. The pattern is vital to the successful completion of your window and must be set up accurately.

Setting Up Your Pattern

1 Use a copier or computer program to enlarge the circular design option you have chosen. The circle should be 10 $^5/_8$ inches in diameter.

Next you will need three additional sheets of paper at least 24 inches by 36 inches: one sheet each of oak tag, carbon paper, and tracing paper (used to create templates for cutting out your glass pieces). Arrange the four sheets in the following order from bottom to top:

- Oak tag
- Carbon paper
- Original pattern
- Tracing paper

2 Secure the four sheets to the work surface with masking tape or pushpins. The papers can be positioned sideways so you do not have to reach so far at subsequent stages.

3 Using a straight edge and a ballpoint pen, trace the outside border lines of the pattern. You must apply moderate pressure to ensure that the lines are transferred by the carbon paper to the oak tag. Sneak a peek at a corner to be sure they are.

PRO TIP ✔

To trace accurately, try resting the bottom of your hand on the work surface for added support as you pull the pen toward you. And go slowly until you develop a rhythm that suits you. Every step in the process is important, starting with pattern preparation.

4 Trace over all the pattern lines of the design.

5 If you are using jewels in the project, place each jewel on the pattern and trace around it. This will assure that the openings for the jewels are the proper size.

6 Pull up a few tabs of tape or pins in the area where the circular insert will be placed.

preparing the large panel project • **85**

7 Slide the insert under the tracing paper and center it within the inner circle of the larger design, making sure it is straight.

8 Reattach the pattern to the work surface.

9 Trace the circular insert.

The entire pattern should now be traced.

Three pieces of information will be included on each piece of the pattern:
- A number to help you position each piece of glass after it has been cut.
- A slash line that indicates the grain direction you want to use for each piece of glass.
- A color designation that corresponds to a particular color of glass.

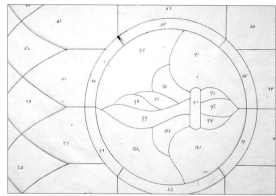

10 Number each piece of the project. This step is intended to assist you in quickly locating each piece of glass as it is added to the project. For this project, we started numbering in the bottom left corner and proceeded left to right, and back again in a zigzag fashion. The inside circle was saved until last.

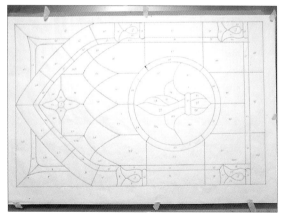

As you number, it's easy to miss a piece and throw off your sequence. If you do this, no problem! Simply label the skipped piece with the same number that it is next to and add a letter (we used B: see our 35B and 49B).

11 The other pieces of information you want on your pattern (slashes for positioning and color-coding) can be indicated with one symbol.

Choose a colored pencil that represents the outside border color. Decide on the direction you want the glass grain to run. Draw a slash mark that represents both color and grain direction. Repeat for all the outside border pieces. We've decided to have the grain run across the short sides of all border pieces.

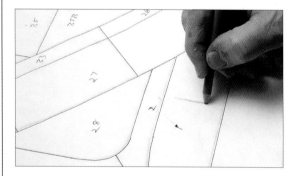

12 With another colored pencil, do the same for the inside border pieces.

13 Do the same for the upper and lower backgrounds.

14 Do the same for all remaining pieces, including the inner circle. The pattern is ready.

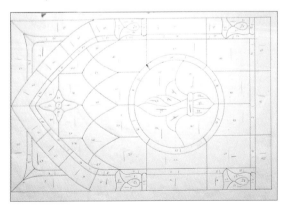

Cutting Out the Pattern

1 Remove all the tape tabs or pushpins. The top, traced copy will be cut apart to create templates for cutting the glass. The original pattern should be retained for your pattern file (Who knows? You might get a request from a neighbor to build a window someday). The carbon paper can be reused several times. You will lay out the panel on top of the oak tag.

2 With regular scissors, cut the tracing paper copy along the outside border, removing the excess paper. Remember—each stage of pattern development is important, so cut as accurately as possible.

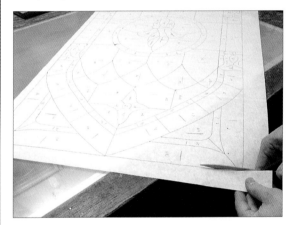

Before you cut the pattern apart, you need to decide which method—lead or foil—you will be using to build the panel. With pattern shears designated for the specific method you choose, cut out the individual pattern pieces. With such a large pattern, it is wise to first cut the design into several more-manageable sections. (Remember to keep the shears to the outside of the line when you cut out spaces for the jewels.)

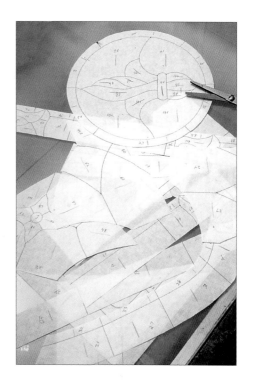

3 Cut out all the pattern pieces and separate them by their color designations.

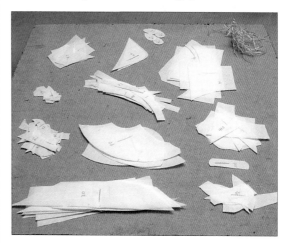

PRO TIPS ✔

If you haven't used pattern shears before or they are giving you trouble, here are a few helpful hints:

1 First, it's helpful to understand how your shears work. Pattern shears have three blades. The single, or top, blade pushes paper from the pattern through the bottom two blades as you cut.

The thin strand of paper that comes out of the lead shears is about the same size as the heart of the lead. Foil shears create a narrower strip of the pattern to allow for copper foil. The result is that each piece of glass will be slightly smaller than the original design. This helps prevent the project from "growing" as you put it together.

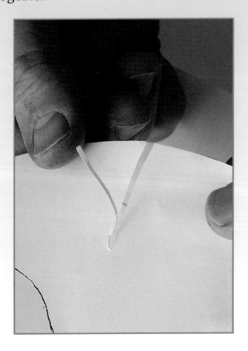

2 As you begin cutting the pattern, open the shears wide and cut down no more than an inch.

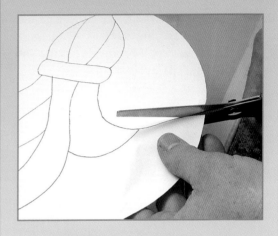

3 Stop, open the shears, and push them up to the point where you stopped at the previous cut.

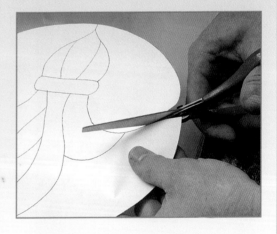

Proceed, cutting no more than an inch at a time.

4 Occasionally, the shears will bend down a section of a line rather than cutting through it.

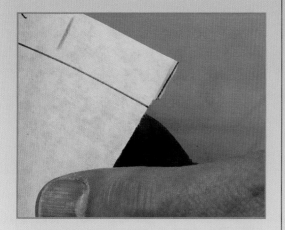

Cut this off with your regular scissors.

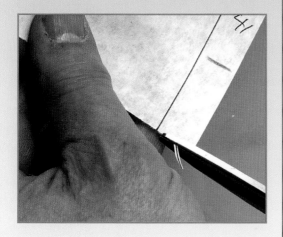

5 When cutting out for pre-cut glass pieces such as jewels or bevels, you cannot cut down the center of the line since it will create a space too small for the glass. Instead, shade the pattern shears to the outside of the jewel or bevel, cutting away the line, but no more.

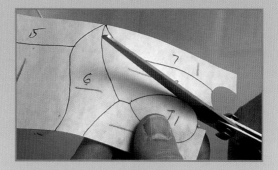

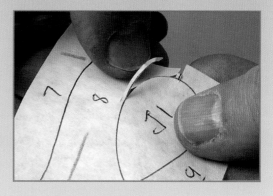

6 When your pattern shears get jammed with paper, rapidly click them together a few times and the excess paper will fall out.

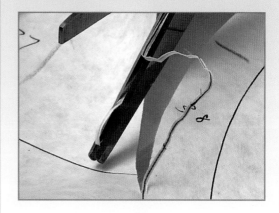

7 It is not a big problem if you are cutting off center a bit. However, make every effort to be as accurate as possible.

Attaching Pattern Pieces to the Glass

One cardinal rule of glass cutting is that you want to cut on the smoother side of the glass. If both sides appear to be equally smooth, use either side.

If you decide that the rough side of the glass is to be on the front of the project, turn over the pattern pieces for that particular glass and attach them upside down on the smooth side of the glass.

1 To attach each pattern piece, apply rubber cement to the perimeter and secure it to the glass.

2 Go through and attach all the pattern pieces to their respective glass selections. Be sure to line up the color slash lines with the grain of the glass.

PRO TIP ✔

In an effort to conserve glass, it is useful to position pattern pieces according to their general shapes. This makes it easy to separate pieces and keeps waste to a minimum. Remember to leave about $^1/_2$ inch between pieces.

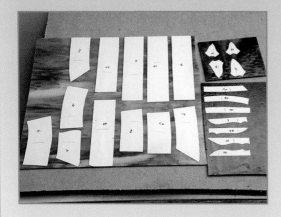

You will notice that some parts of a typical sheet of glass might be more or less interesting than others due to heavier color concentration, unique markings, bubbles, roller marks, color striations, and so on. A light box is useful for selecting specific glass areas that will enhance your project. And remember: What one person might see as a flaw in the glass can often be more aptly described as a unique characteristic.

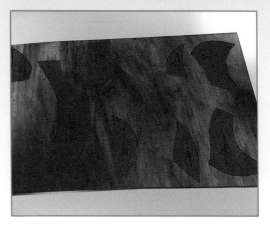

Cutting the Glass

Remember another cardinal rule of cutting: Take out the inside curves first.

We'll start with the pieces that are probably the most difficult ones in the project to cut. If you do them successfully, the rest should be a breeze.

1 Draw three arcs, score, and break each arc from the inside curve of piece 91.

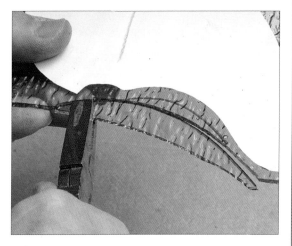

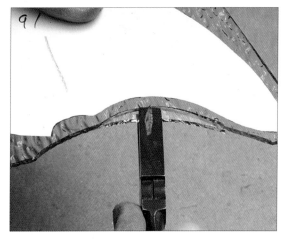

2 Cut out an arc in the small curve. The remaining arc should be about $^1/_4$ inch all around.

3 Cut out the remaining arc, using the pliers at the angle shown here to pull the glass loose.

4 Cut out the remaining section of the larger inside curve in two pieces.

5 Remove the glass from the two remaining convex curves in any order you want.

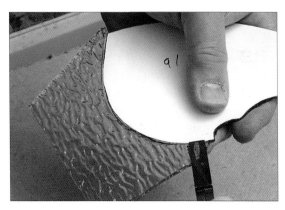

6 The second piece we'll cut (piece number 64) is part of the thin circular border in the center. There are six of these. We first indicate the small arcs to be trimmed away.

7 Remove two arcs, leaving about $1/4$ inch.

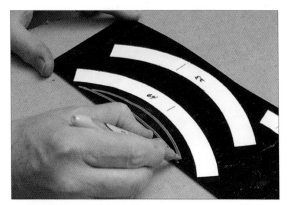

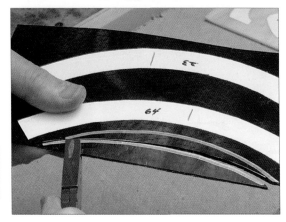

10
Remove the rest of the excess glass and groze any burrs that might remain.

8
Starting at either end, remove about a third of the remaining arc.

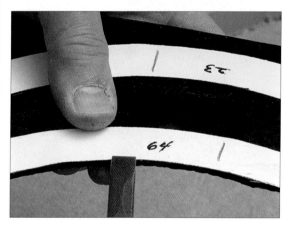

9
Remove another part of the arc from the opposite end.

11
Separate the piece you are working on from the uncut piece adjacent to it. Cut as straight a line as possible.

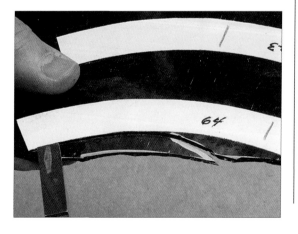

12 Cut off both short ends

13 Cut the remaining convex arc and remove.

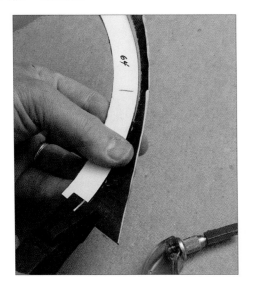

The third piece we're tackling is one side of the area that holds the pear-shaped jewel (piece number 80). This is a tricky piece, and there are eight to cut.

14 Start by drawing two arcs in the deeper curve as shown. Cut the first arc.

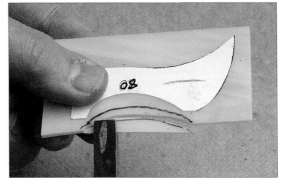

15 Cut the second arc.

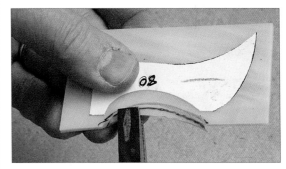

16 Starting at either end, score about half of the remaining arc and remove it.

17 Score the rest of the arc and remove it.

18 Because this piece has back-to-back curves, the main stress point is the narrowest point, where the two curves meet. After the first curve is cut, the second should be taken out in pieces as well. Start by removing a gentle curve, as shown.

19 Remove another arc as shown, leaving about $^1/_4$ inch of glass.

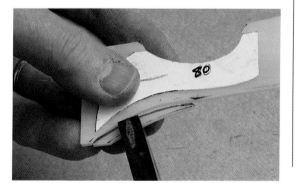

20 Cut the remaining glass by scoring along the pattern edge about halfway and graduating your score toward the outside.

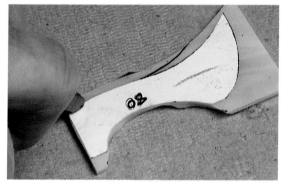

21 Cut the remaining arc.

22 Cut the rest of the glass from the piece.

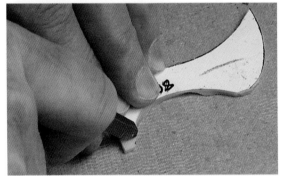

Grinding the Glass

If you are working with lead came, it is not necessary to have perfectly smooth edges on your glass. But if excess glass protrudes past the pattern edge, it needs to be removed. Likewise, if some areas have sharp edges, you will want to dull those with a stone or grinder to avoid cutting yourself during the leading process. If you're working with copper foil, it's more important to grind the edges of the glass so the adjoining pieces fit tightly.

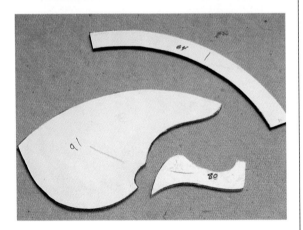

If you were able to cut these pieces pretty closely, you should not have much trouble with the other 100-plus pieces.

23 Cut all the remaining glass now.

8

Completing a Large Leaded Panel

I F CONSTRUCTED CORRECTLY, THE PANEL YOU
are about to make can be expected to last for 75 to
100 years without a great deal of maintenance. Your
legacy as a stained glass artist might very well be at
stake—so take your time and build your panel well.

The copy of the pattern that was made on the oak tag
is your project's blueprint. The lines closely approxi-
mate where the lead cames will go and the glass should
fit. It is important to get this set up properly.

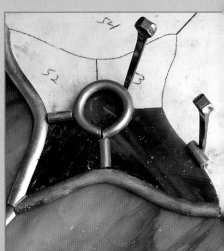

Preparing the Pattern

1 With regular scissors, cut along the outside lines of the pattern, removing the excess oak tag.

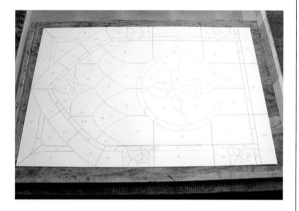

2 Cut four 1-inch-long pieces of the came you are using for the outside border and set them aside. (We are using $^1/_4$-inch flat H-lead)

3 Place the oak tag in the bottom left corner of the lead board. Pull it away about $^1/_8$ inch from both sides of the corner.

Set a 1-inch piece of the H-lead against the bottom edge of the lead board.

4 Insert the bottom left piece of glass (looking at the pattern sideways, with the top of the panel to your left) in it and place another piece of lead on the opposite edge of the glass.

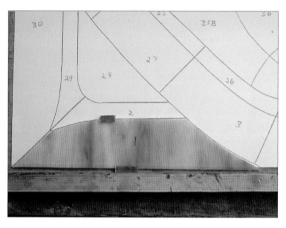

5 If necessary, reposition the oak tag until the heart of the top piece of lead is directly over the pattern line.

6 Repeat the lead and glass placement for the top left piece of glass as shown.

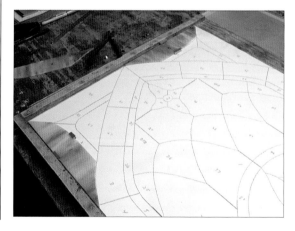

7 Position the oak tag as necessary.

8 Add two additional pieces of glass with lead scraps, as shown.

9 This is the proper position for the oak tag pattern. To keep it in place, secure it with several pieces of masking tape.

Stretching Lead

Lead usually comes in 6-foot strips. You should store your lead so it remains flat and relatively straight. Don't let it twist or develop kinks. It's a good idea to transport lead in a long cardboard box (when you buy lead, ask your stained glass store for one) or a section of PVC pipe.

Before you start fitting the lead, each strip must be stretched. This will straighten the lead and make it firmer.

1 Using a lead stretcher secured to your workbench, insert about 1 inch of the lead strip and secure it by pushing down on the stretcher. The serrated jaws will hold the lead in place.

2 With your breaking pliers, take hold of the opposite end of the lead and squeeze it tight. Position your feet sideways so that if the lead should break during stretching you will not fall backwards. Now tug on the lead. You should see the lead straightening as it is being stretched. Once it is straight, you're done. You should stretch only one piece, or maybe two, at a time.

Leading the Project

As you begin adding pieces of lead, remember that you always need to start with lead that has a cleanly cut end rather than a crimped end. You achieve this by having the flat edges of the pliers facing the piece that you want to use.

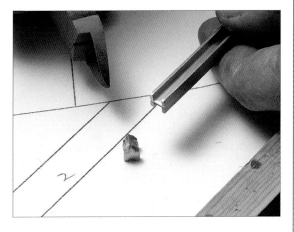

1 Long pieces of lead should be cut to form the bottom and left borders of the project. Place an end of lead along the bottom of the board and push it against the left side.

2 Scratch a mark where the lead intersects the pattern line on the opposite end and cut it off.

3 Secure the lead on the outside with a nail.

4 Place a length of lead up the left side in the same fashion. It will butt up against the first lead.

The first piece of glass to be inserted is number 1.

5 Remove the paper pattern and position the piece in the bottom lead channel.

PRO TIP ✔

It is important to keep the longer strips of lead from bending too much as you work with them. In this project, you will discover that most of the lead pieces you will be working with are less than 12 inches long. Instead of cutting from the 6-foot pieces, cut them into more manageable 2- to 3-foot lengths.

6 Secure piece 1 with a nail. Bend a piece of the lead that you are using in the interior of the project (we used $1/4$-inch rounded H-lead), to the contour of piece 1. Overlap it about $1/2$ inch to the left.

7 Scratch a line showing the angle where the lead meets the pattern line that is to the left of the glass. Note that this is the sharpest angle you will need to cut in the project, and you will need to use the lead knife.

8 Rock your knife back and forth several times while pushing down. As you break through the top leaf, push straight down through the heart until you reach the bottom leaf. Repeat the back and forth rocking until you cut through the lead.

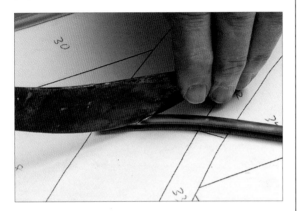

Because of the sharp angle, one or both tips of the lead may get bent a little. If this happens, straighten them with your lead knife.

9 Nail a scrap piece of lead on the left side of the glass and check the fit of the angle.

10 Scratch a line for the angle on the right side of piece number 1. This lead will not go clear to the end of the glass but to where it would meet an intersecting lead as represented by the scrap piece already in place. Note that we have used the lead knife to scratch the angle to be cut. You might find this easier than using a nail.

11 Check for proper fit.

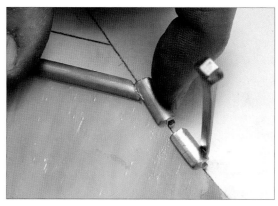

PRO TIP ✔

Whenever you get a piece of lead set, hold it securely in place with a nail.

When you get a piece of glass set, use a scrap lead between the glass and nail to avoid chipping.

12 Insert piece number 2 in place and secure it with a nail. Use an arrow cut to position the lead in the corner. Use a lead scrap to determine the angle for cutting the other end of the lead. Check for a proper fit.

13 Position pieces 30 and 29 in the same way

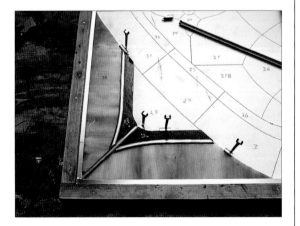

14 Bend a piece of lead around the curved edges of piece number 28. Note that overlapping the lead by $1/2$ inch or so will allow you to more easily bend the lead.

15 Both ends of the lead will be cut short to allow for an intersecting lead. Hold the piece in place with three nails and determine the angles to be cut by using a lead scrap. Then cut both sides with a knife.

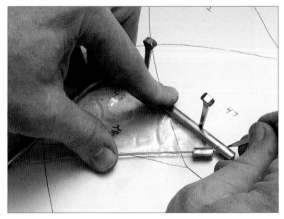

16 Remove the nails holding the corner pieces and insert the newly cut lead and glass.

17 Tap the glass lightly with your hammer to be sure it is seated completely. Secure it with a nail.

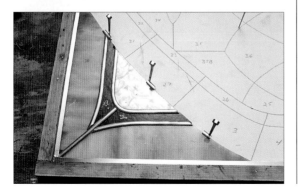

18 Bend a length of lead to the general contour of the five-piece corner section. Miter both ends so they meet evenly with the outside border leads and secure.

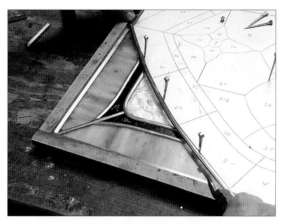

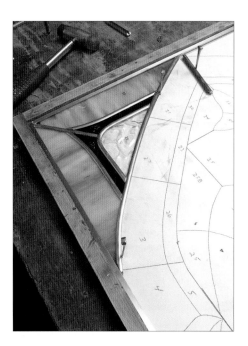

20 Add pieces 3, 27, and 71 with short leads. Then add a longer lead that covers the four previously placed glass pieces. This will be cut short to allow for intersecting leads on both ends.

19 Continue with piece 4 and a short lead.

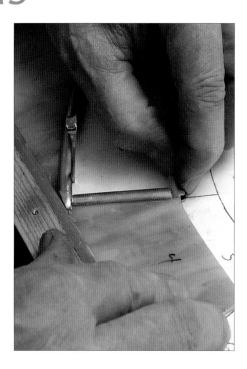

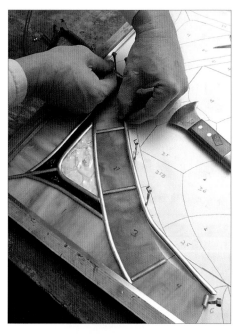

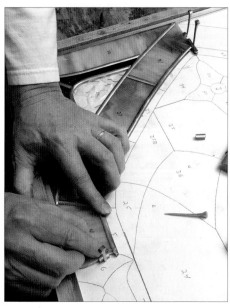

21 Add the thin border pieces 5, 26, 33, and 32.

Because we used $^3/_{16}$-inch lead for the inside of the thin border, it was important to use a $^3/_{16}$-inch lead scrap when measuring for the short connecting leads.

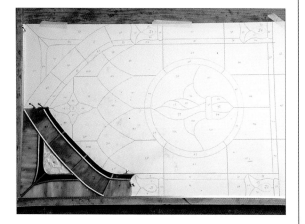

22 With the next piece of lead, we started using $^3/_{16}$-inch H-round since the five pieces in each of the "pedestal" sections are small and curved. The smaller lead, while offering some variety, is easier to bend. Cut the first lead and tap in piece 6.

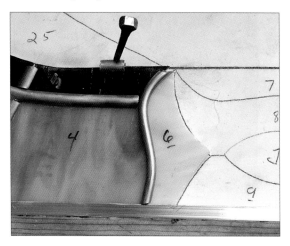

23 Add a lead between pieces 6 and 9 and tap in piece 9.

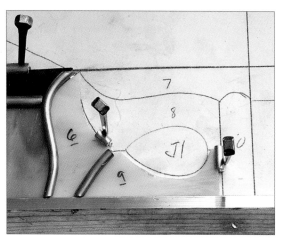

Wrapping lead around the pear-shaped jewels is a little tricky. Learn the first one well since you will have three more to do. (Additional information on this is offered in chapter 4, pages 62 and 63.)

24 Start by mitering one end of the lead at the top point, then wrap it around the jewel, extending it past the miter about 3 inches.

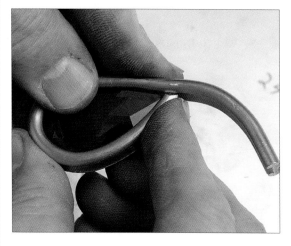

25 Set the wrapped jewel against piece 9 and push the extended lead against piece 6. Miter it using a scrap of the $^1/_4$-inch lead.

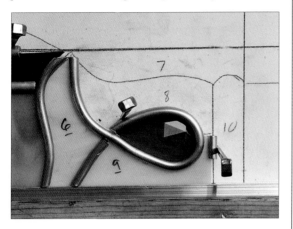

26 When you add pieces 10 and 11, notice that the lead that is placed on the outer edge of piece 8 requires the lead extending up from the pear jewel to be altered with an arrow miter.

At this point, two issues need to be addressed: As seen in the photo, the end of the lead on 10 that touches the border lead is too short. It needs to be replaced. And the small gap between 10 and the red jewel is too small for a piece of lead. We will show you the solution when we start soldering.

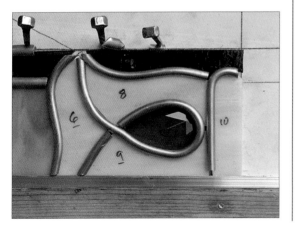

27 Continue adding, in order, pieces 12, 11, 14, and 13. Any time a lead that is in place needs to be moved, use a lathken or fid to tap it into place. Also note that we resumed using the $^1/_4$-inch lead at the bottom of the pedestal.

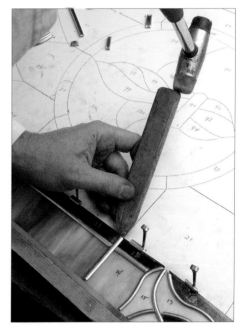

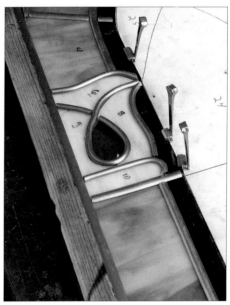

28 Build the second five-piece pedestal section and border piece 18 the same way you did the previous pedestal.

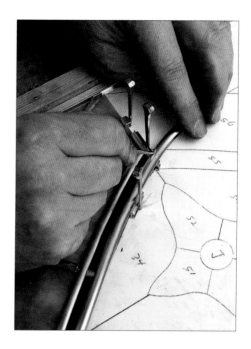

29 With the left side of the double border section completed, now add a dominant lead that gets mitered at the apex of the arch.

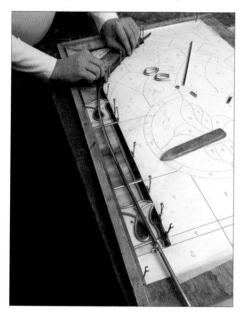

30 Continue pushing the lead against the border pieces and insert nails every 6 inches or so. When you reach the bottom of the border section, use a 1/4-inch lead scrap to determine where it is to be cut.

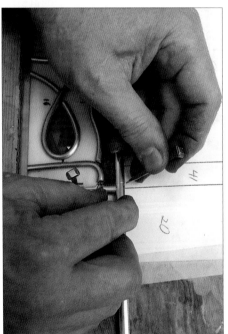

31 To cut the lead, pull it away from the glass, hold the lead pliers vertically and snip. Your lead knife will work fine as well.

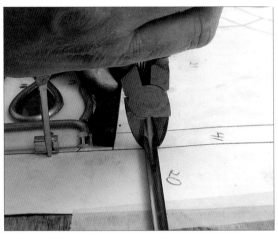

Nail it securely.

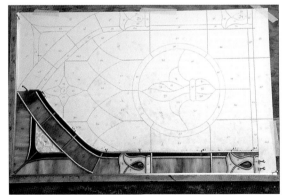

32 The sequence continues with piece 25, a short lead, piece 35B, and a long lead.

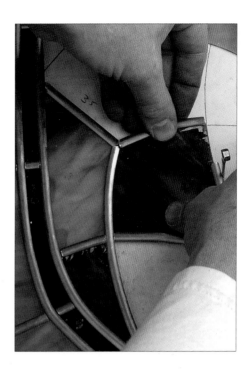

33 Piece 24 is next, then a long lead and piece 36. This section finishes with a short lead on piece 35 that gets mitered against the border (you will need the lead knife for this miter) and has an arrow miter where it converges with two leads from piece 36.

Remember to tap the glass pieces so that they sit tightly against the leads.

34 The next piece is 35. Ours is a bit too large.

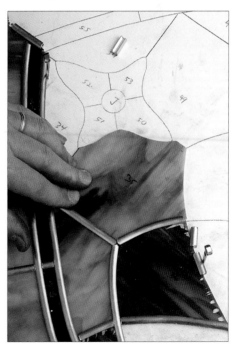

Fixing this problem is easy. Mark the areas where it is to be trimmed. Groze or grind to fit.

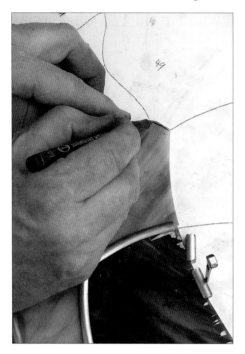

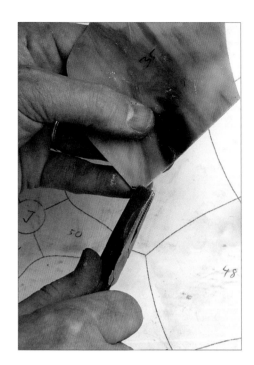

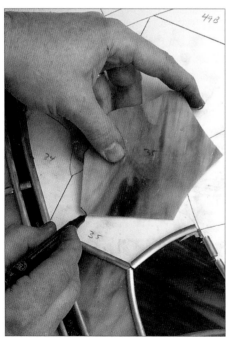

35 Add piece 34. Then start the star with pieces 52 and 51. Wrap the circular jewel as detailed in the lead primer chapter and insert it, making sure the seam is against one of the small leads that separate the first two star parts. Note the miters at the star points.

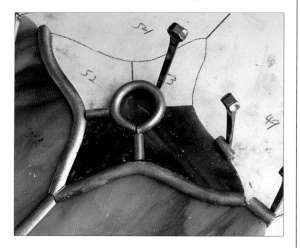

36 Add the two additional star pieces.

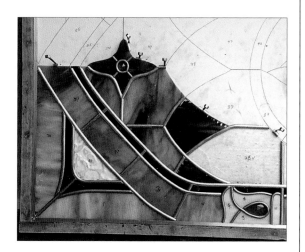

37 Add pieces 37, 22, 21, and 40. This creates half the circle to set the stage for forming the center medallion.

38 Take a piece of lead at least 14 inches long and gently bend it to the shape of half the circle. Overlap it on both ends $1/2$ inch or more.

39 Mark the left end of the lead. It should start in the middle of the lead that is placed along piece 37.

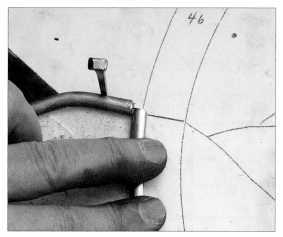

40
Continue bending the lead and pushing it onto the glass around the circle. Nail the lead every 6 inches or so.

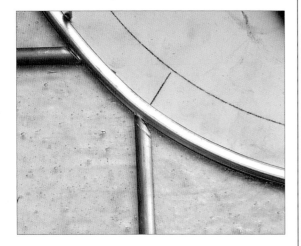

Note: In the photo above, the angle of the lead that meets the circle is off enough that it should be replaced.

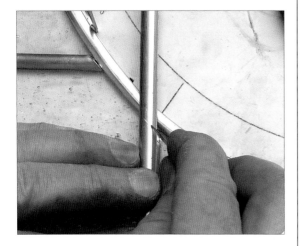

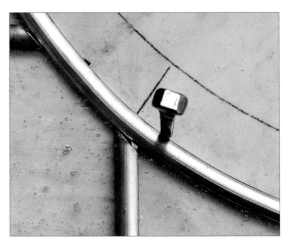

41
Mark and cut the right end of the lead the same way as when you started the circle.

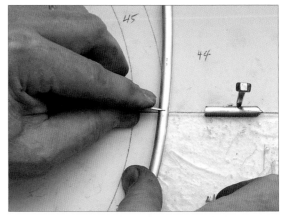

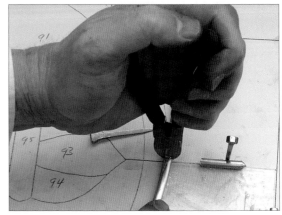

42 Place the three border pieces 38, 23, and 39 from left to right and add a half circle of lead.

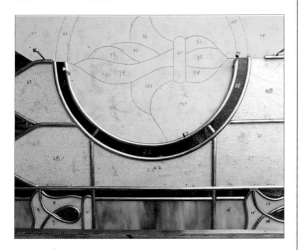

43 For the medallion, start with piece 101 (Note that we switched back to $^3/_{16}$-inch H-lead). Then add a piece of lead that bends around the left side from the border to the oval (piece 95), and add piece 102.

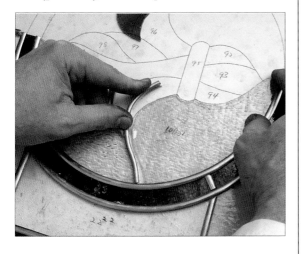

44 Add a small piece of lead that joins pieces 102 and 100. Insert piece 100.

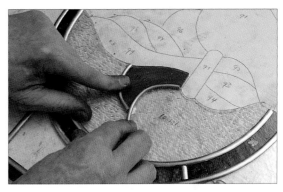

45 Insert a lead that covers pieces 102 and 100. Insert piece 99 and cap it with a lead. Continue tapping in the glass with the hammer.

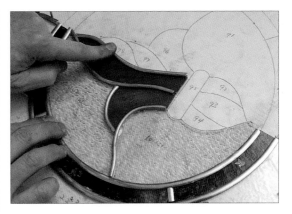

46 Continue with pieces 98 and 97. Be sure to cut accurate miters.

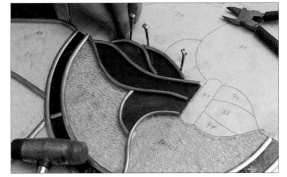

PRO TIPS ✔

1 As you hold the leads in place, be sure the nails are put in vertically and not slanted. If you inadvertently drive a nail through the bottom flange of the lead, it produces a hole on the other side.

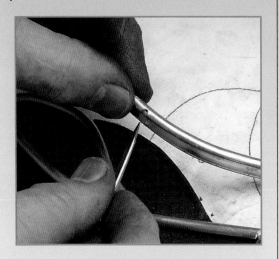

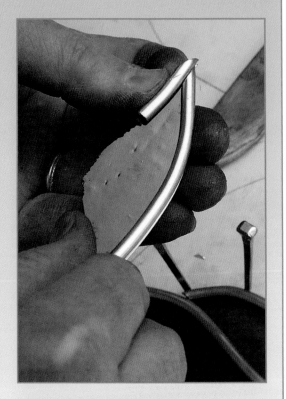

2 When you are cutting a sharp angle, hold a scrap lead where a lead needs to be mitered. It might be easier to see the exact angle.

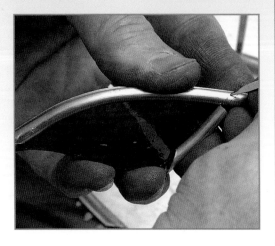

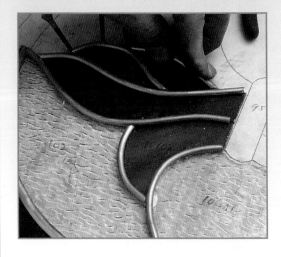

The dark oval piece that separates the flame (piece 95) gets completely wrapped in lead. Lay it in its place and mark a spot where it will meet an abutting lead. This is where you will start the lead on piece 95.

48 Bend the lead tightly around the glass and miter the end.

Set it in place.

49 Continue with pieces 94, 93, 92, 97, and 96.

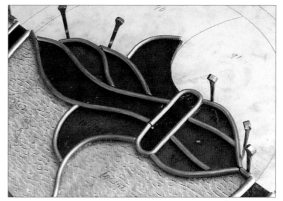

50 Add pieces 90 and 91. You will probably need to tap these in to set them properly. Add the half circle of lead, the three remaining border pieces, and the outer half circle of lead. About 60 percent of the leading is now complete.

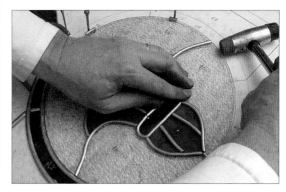

Our piece 49 is a bit too large, so we will groze or grind it to fit.

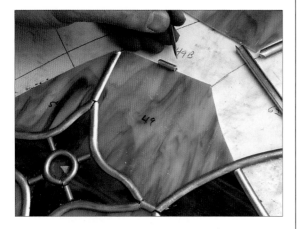

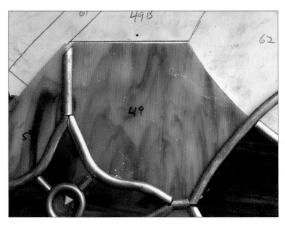

51 Continue with the remaining pieces that fit inside the small arched border.

52 Miter the long lead that will extend from the top of the star. Secure it with a nail.

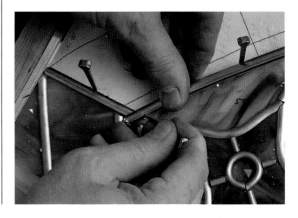

53 Bend the lead around the arch toward the bottom of the panel. Add additional nails and let it extend past the bottom of the pattern. This will be cut later.

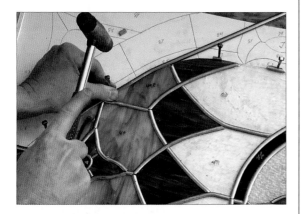

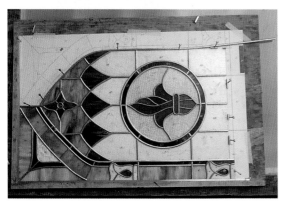

54 Nail a lead scrap to the outside bottom of piece 66.

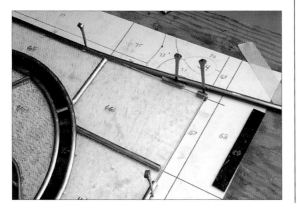

55 Cut a lead that will extend across the four clear pieces.

56 Add the three dark, small border pieces (41, 42 and 67).

57 Cut the bottom of the larger lead piece that started up by the star. Use a scrap lead to measure where it meets the dominant horizontal lead. Nail it in place.

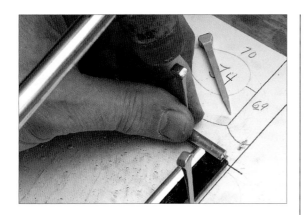

59 Complete the remaining pieces of the border, including the two pedestals. Hold all pieces in place with nails.

58 Add the first four pieces of the inside and outside borders of the arch using the same approach you used on the opposite side. Add the five pieces that make up the top right corner.

60 Lay in the last wide border pieces (20, 43, and 68).

61 Attach outside border leads to the two exposed sides of the panel.

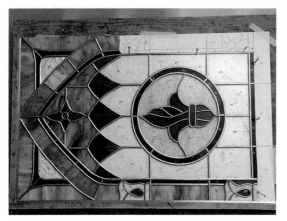

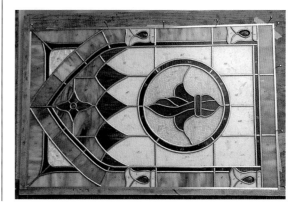

Soldering the Panel

Hopefully, most of your lead joints are mitered closely.

For ones that have some spaces, we will address a few remedies prior to soldering (see the Pro Tips on the next two pages).

1 Go through the panel and fill any lead gaps. A $1/32$-inch gap probably does not matter too much, but a $1/16$-inch gap does matter and should be filled.

The joint shown here should have had a sliver added so the solder would have had a proper bridge.

2 Apply flux to all the joints. As you take flux from the bottle, clean off the excess so you do not apply too much to the first few joints.

PRO TIPS ✔

1 Small lead slivers can be cut as fillers when there is a gap between leads.

Cut a section from the top of the lead that will fit snugly in the gap you are filling. Push it into place with a nail.

Take a short length of lead and cut down the center of the heart. Lift the top of the lead (leaf).

2 Another technique for filling gaps is to cut partway through the upper leaf of the lead by rocking the knife back and forth until the lead is cut through about $1/16$ inch. Push the lead forward until it meets the adjoining lead.

3 Sometimes you can move a point of a mitered lead with your lead knife.

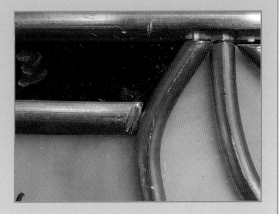

3 Plug in your soldering iron and allow it to heat up. The proper heat level is achieved when the solder melts instantly when touched to the tip, and the iron can rest on the lead for a two second count without melting the lead. Insure that both of these conditions are met before you start soldering by testing on some scrap lead.

4 Lay the solder on the lead joint and put your iron down on the solder, melting it and allowing it to flow across the joint. Your iron should move only enough to spread the solder to the joints. As the solder melts, lift the solder spool out of the way. You will use about $^1/_8$ inch of solder on most joints.

The solder print should be mostly flat and cover the joint in a generally symmetrical pattern. Leads that meet at a right angle should have T-shaped joints.

PRO TIP: FIXING SOLDER JOINTS

1 When joints do not have enough solder to make a "T", add additional solder.

2 When joints have too much solder, remelt the joint and pull some solder off onto the iron's tip. Remove the excess solder. Set the iron back down and allow the solder to melt again.

5 Solder from left to right along the panel. If you need to, turn the panel around for easier access to the upper section.

6 Solder all the lead joints on the front side.

7 Remove all nails in the board and get ready to turn the panel over.

8 Slide the panel along the edge of your table, supporting it as you move it to a position perpendicular to the floor.

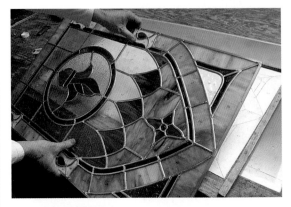

9 Set the bottom edge of the panel on the floor and rotate the panel 180 degrees.

11 Look over the panel and fill any lead joints that appear to be short.

10 Raise the panel along the edge of the table to avoid flexing it. Lay it down gently and push it onto the table.

12 Flux all the joints and solder as you did on the front side.

NOTE: If at any time while soldering you get a solder blob as shown below, it's because you have too little or no flux.

The remedy is to apply flux and re-melt the solder.

There is an old axiom in the annals of stained glass: No matter how often you check, there will always be at least one lead joint that does not get soldered. Do you want to look over the panel one more time?

Cementing

When you moved or turned the panel over, you might have heard some glass clinking or felt some bending of the lead. The panel is still not stable and must be cemented. The cement will also weatherproof the panel, making it suitable for installing in an opening where it will face the elements. We used Inland's pre-mixed cement system.

Although some veteran leaded glass artists don't bother, we like to get 95 percent of the flux off the lead and glass before cementing.

1 With a sponge and a mild detergent, wash off the flux and dry the panel thoroughly.

2 Spread out newspaper or an alternative since this is a messy job.

3 Once you open the container, you might notice that some of the oil has separated from the powder. Pour the oil in a larger, separate container.

4 Using a screwdriver or other similar device, break up a portion of the hardened cement and put it in the container with the oil.

5 Repeat for the remaining cement in the container.

6 Continue mixing the cement until it reaches a smooth consistency.

7 Pour a portion of the cement around the various sections of the panel. Plan on using about half your supply, or a little bit more.

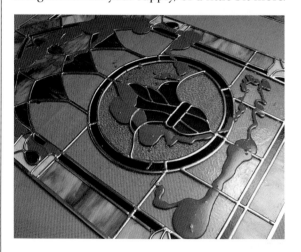

8 Using a small scrub brush, work the cement into the lead cames by brushing it perpendicular to the leads.

9 Remove most of the excess by moving it along the lead and put it back into the container.

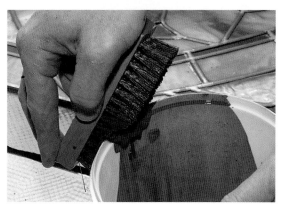

10 Use a small cup or jar to sprinkle a coating of whiting on the panel.

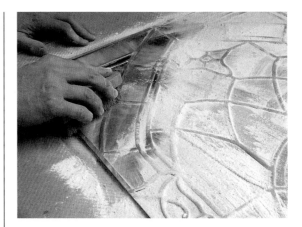

11 Brush the whiting in against the lead cames so it makes contact with the cement.

12 Using a back-and-forth motion, scrub the leads lengthwise. You will need to be a bit vigorous with this, but not so much that you break the glass.

PRO TIP ✔

The whiting has three functions:

1 It will soak up the oils from the cement, cleaning the glass.

2 It will help the cement set up and harden.

3 As you scrub the lead, the whiting and cement will cause the channels to darken.

13 With a bench brush, brush off the majority of the powder and turn the panel over.

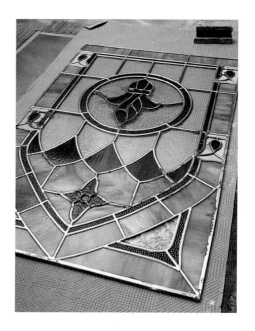

14 Repeat steps 7 through 13 and allow the panel to sit for 24 hours. (Letting it sit for 48 hours will not hurt, but no more than that.) Clean up your mess and take a break until tomorrow.

15 Using the point of a plastic fid or sharpened $1/4$-inch dowel, run along the edges of all the leads, cleaning away any cement that may have seeped out of the cames.

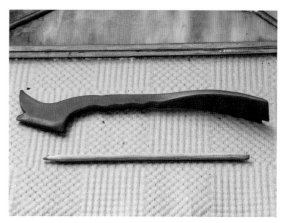

17 Now do a final scrubbing of the lead with your cement brush to eliminate any scratches and to even out any color differences.

16 Use a bench brush to remove the powder you produced.

Now have someone hold the panel upright for you. Enjoy your creation!

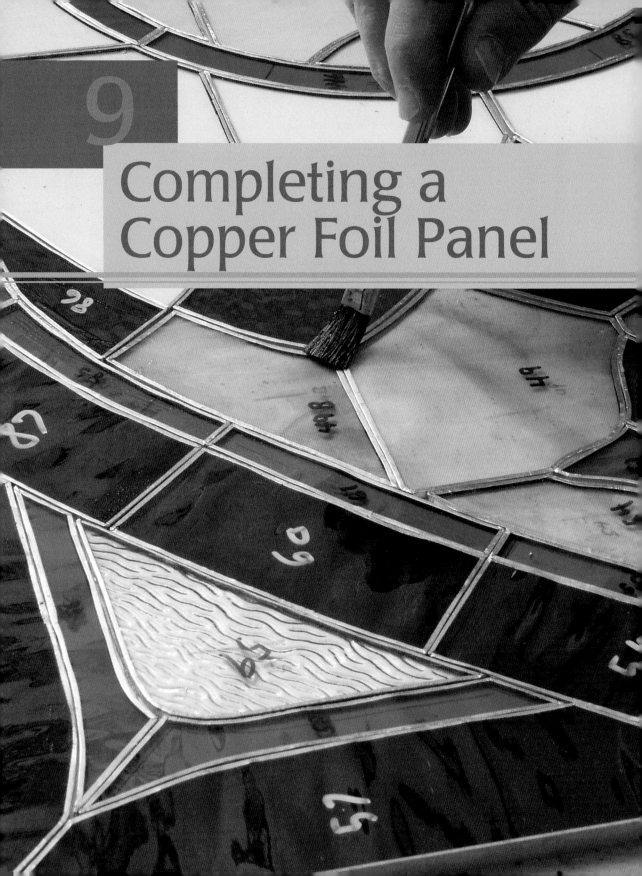

9

Completing a Copper Foil Panel

J OINING PIECES OF COLORED GLASS BY WRAP-
ping the edges in copper and then melting solder
along the seams is a process that dates back to the
mid-1800s. John Lafarge and Louis Comfort Tiffany are
the two individuals who are given the most credit for
developing the copper foil method for building stained
glass windows.

Pins
___
abeza

Cleaning the Glass

In order for the foil to adhere properly, the glass must be thoroughly cleaned. Prepare two wash basins, one with warm soapy water (we use a product called Simple Green) and the other with plain warm water for rinsing.

1 After removing the pattern paper from a piece, wash the glass with a sponge. Run the sponge around the edges, removing the dust created from grinding.

2 Rinse the glass in warm water and dry on a towel.

3 Write the pattern number on the piece

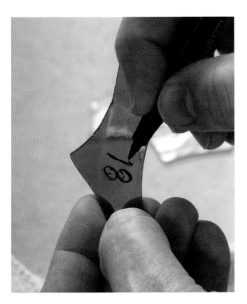

4 Wash, dry, and number all of the pieces.

Fitting the Glass

1 With all the glass pieces cut and ground, we want to make sure they all fit together properly on the pattern. Place the oak tag copy of the design on your work board and attach lay-out strips with pushpins along the bottom and left side. Put them directly on the outside pattern lines.

Remember those pattern shears? The paper strip that was removed represented the space taken up by the copper foil. You cannot forget that as we lay out the pieces to check the proper fitting.

In this step we will use glass-headed straight pins as spacers between the pieces of glass to represent the foil.

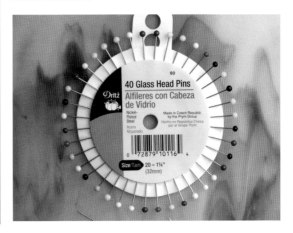

2 Start by locating the first few pieces of glass that make up the bottom left corner. Lay piece 30 against the layout strip. Insert two pins toward the top and bottom of the long curved side. The pins should be on the pattern line.

3 Insert piece number 1 against the bottom layout strip. Place pins on the straight seam that separates the two pieces as well as on the curved side of piece 1.

You should see the pattern line at the outer ends of both pieces 30 and 1. If glass covers the line at either point, it needs to be ground down a bit.

Note: If you groze or grind any pieces, be sure to wash them again.

As you proceed, if some pieces appear to be a little small, don't worry about it; just don't let the pieces be too large, which will result in the panel growing in size.

4 Continue with pieces 2, 29, and 28.

If there are any points where glass touches glass when the pins are in place, these should be ground down. You should be able to see a consistent spacing between all pieces.

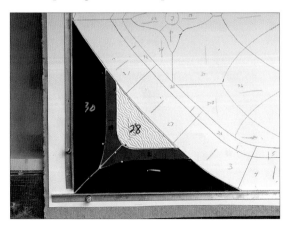

5 Notice how piece 10 is pushing against piece 7, even without a pin between them.

We grozed piece 10 along its short straight edge until it fit properly and a pin could fit between the two pieces.

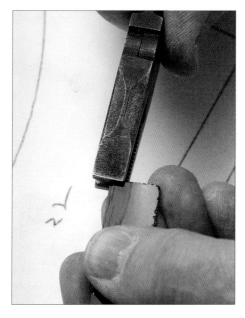

6 Continue fitting the remaining pieces.

NOTE: So you do not have to use hundreds of pins, you can remove some of the pins from earlier stages and use them in new areas. Two packs of forty pins should be enough.

PRO TIP ✔

When you have all the pieces fitted properly, check to see if any of the glass pieces have scratches or undesirable marks.

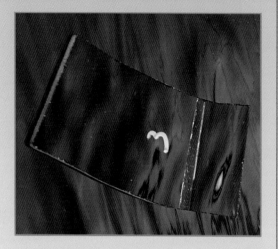

1 To replace a piece, put the original on top of a like piece of glass and line up the grain direction.

2 Trace around the original piece with a glass marker.

3 Cut the glass on the inside of the marker line. Grind as needed and wash. Set the new piece in the design.

Foiling the Glass

Solder does not adhere to glass, so each piece must be wrapped in copper foil, a metal that can be soldered. Copper foil comes in 36-yard rolls and many different widths (we used $^7/_{32}$-inch, a mid-sized foil). It has adhesive on the back and is attached to a waste paper that peels off as the foil is applied. There are also three different colors of foil backing: copper, black, and silver. When clear or light shades of transparent glass are used, the back of the foil can be seen through the glass. Since we planned to apply black patina to the solder seams, black-backed foil was chosen so that it would blend in.

1 Remove the glass-headed pins. Remove the pins holding the layout strips.

2 Push the layout strips up and to the right, moving the entire panel 2 or 3 inches in both directions. This will allow you easy access to the pieces as you apply the copper foil.

3 Start with pattern piece number 30. Peel back several inches of foil backing with the underside or sticky side of the foil facing you. Center the glass and attach it to the end of the foil.

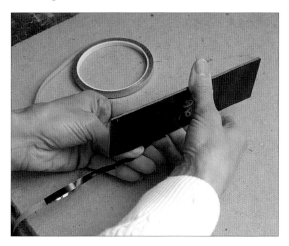

Since the solder will only flow onto the foil, it is important to get the foil as even as possible

4 Pull the foil taut and attach it evenly to the glass.

5 Rotate the glass toward you and push the foil onto the short side of the glass.

6 Continue applying the foil and overlap it about $1/8$ inch when you reach the end. Cut it with scissors.

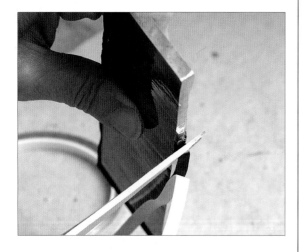

7 With your thumb, push the foil onto the edge of the glass—you are not folding it over the sides of the glass yet.

8 At a corner, fold down one of the top edges (your fingernail is helpful here). Repeat on the bottom edge as well.

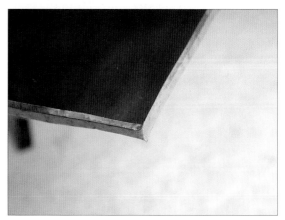

9 Run your thumb and index finger along the long side of the glass, bending the foil over onto the glass.

10 Continue to fold the other three corners and edges.

PRO TIP ✔

There are several machines available that speed up the process of applying foil. The one pictured below is manufactured by Glastar.

11 With a foil finisher or fid, burnish the foil onto the glass.

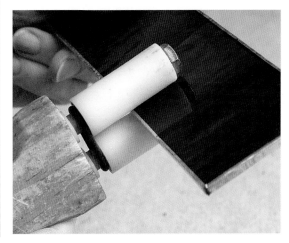

PRO TIP ✔

The piece pictured below has lots of mistakes:

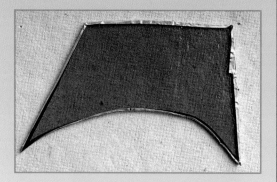

1 The foil is not very even all around. This needs to be redone.

2 The upper right corner was not folded properly. You could overlap a small piece of foil, $1/2$ inch in both directions, and fold as directed.

3 In the lower right corner, the foil was pierced by the glass. The glass should be dulled on a stone and refoiled.

4 The seam where the overlap occurred is not even. With a craft knife, trim off the excess.

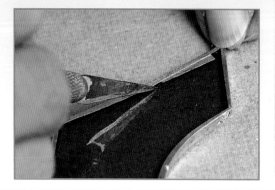

5 The inside arc has two cracked pieces of foil. Wrap pieces of foil over the cracks and extend them onto both sides of the glass.

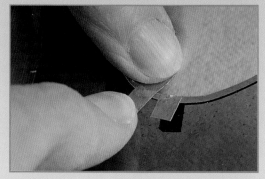

Burnish the foil and trim evenly with a craft knife.

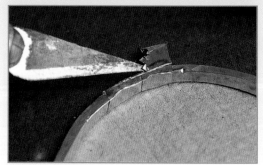

6 The foil is not burnished well in several areas. Use the fid and press a little harder.

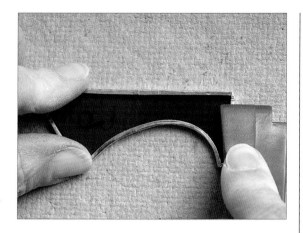

It is not necessary to have every crease completely flattened

12 Replace the piece on the pattern copy.

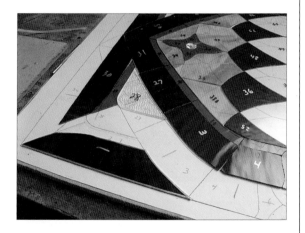

13 Finish foiling all of the pieces.

Soldering the Panel

1 With all of the prep work completed, it is time to put the panel together. Plug in your soldering iron (you should be using a $1/4$-inch to $1/2$-inch wide tip) and soak the sponge with water.

2 Attach layout strips on all four sides of the project.

You will soon notice that the layout strips can interfere with the positioning of your iron. However, they are holding the pieces together as we begin to solder.

To join all the glass, you will apply small amounts of solder to many of the areas where the pieces of glass converge. This is called tack soldering.

3 Apply flux to all of the foil seams.

If you should wind up with a blob of solder, apply a little flux, melt it, and spread it out.

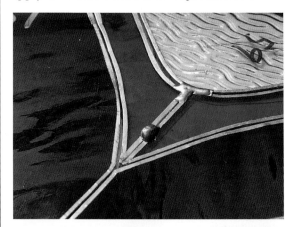

4 Unwind about 6 inches of solder. Set the end on an intersection where three or more pieces of glass meet and melt off about $1/8$ inch of solder with the iron. When the solder melts, lift the solder spool and then lift the iron about one second later. The extra second allows the solder to spread out and ensures that the melted solder will not reattach to the spool.

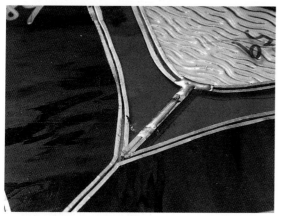

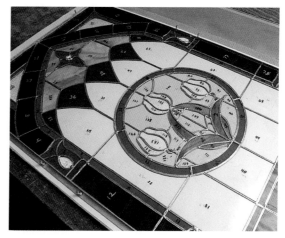

5 Finish tack soldering the rest of the panel.

6 Remove the layout strips and pull out the oak tag pattern copy.

It does not really matter where you start soldering. However, you will want to minimize the distance you reach over the project since most of our backs do not like bending for extended periods. We started soldering a little past the midpoint.

7 As you begin to apply solder to the copper seams, hold the iron like you are shaking hands or holding a sword. The iron should rest on the copper, tilted at a 45-degree angle. The barrel should be parallel to the glass. The solder spool is held in your opposite hand at about a 45-degree angle to the iron. Always pull the iron and solder toward you so that you can see the solder melt.

8 Find a hot point on the iron's tip—this will usually be about half an inch back and toward the bottom or underside. As the solder makes contact with the iron along the seam, continue to feed solder onto the tip. The solder should flow down the tip and onto the copper seam.

9 Continue soldering the panel. The goal is to apply a slightly rounded mound of solder to all of the seams. Be as consistent as possible.

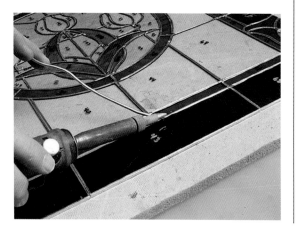

If you're not really comfortable with your soldering skills yet, apply a flat coat of solder first, followed by a beaded coat. This is detailed in chapter 6.

Since solder will flow where the foil is, you have no control over the width of the seam. If the glass fits snugly together initially, the seams will be the same width. Gaps between the glass pieces, while easily filled in, will affect the width of the seams.

PRO TIP ✔

1 To determine whether your iron is at the right temperature, melt a small amount of solder from the spool. If it melts instantly and adheres to the tip, it is in a good range. If it takes time to melt, it is probably too cool. If the solder falls off, it is likely too hot.

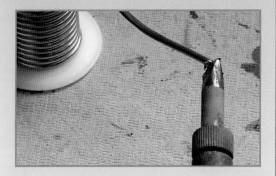

2 If you notice that the solder is spreading onto the glass, flux the area and slowly drag the excess to another area of the panel.

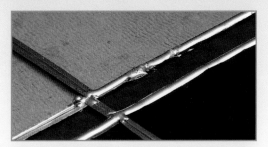

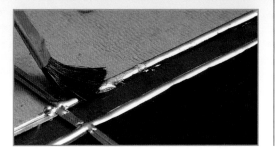

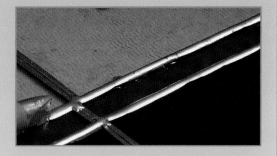

3 If the solder forms a blob rather than flowing onto the copper, you might have missed that area with flux. Flux over top of the solder and remelt with your iron.

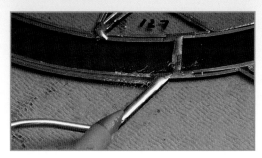

4 If an area of solder is bumpy, flux lightly and remelt the solder.

5 If you decide to stop for the day before the panel is finished, you will need to clean the panel. With a cleaner, attempt to remove about 90 percent of the flux. Flux can corrode the solder if left on and will make future soldering and finishing difficult.

6 If you have a blemish on the solder, put your iron on the area, wait one second, then slowly lift up your iron.

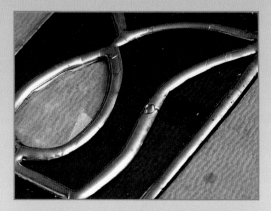

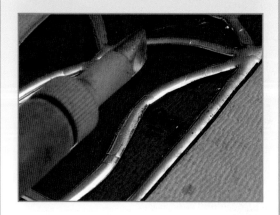

When the front side is completed to your satisfaction, the panel needs to be turned over. However, it is not very stable at this point so you should do it carefully. The main concern here is that the panel not be allowed to flex or bend. This will likely cause pieces of glass to crack.

10 Slide the panel toward the front edge of the table. Support it with your hands on the two long sides.

11 Lift the back edge, causing the panel to be raised in a vertical position, supported by your front hand. Set it vertically on the work board.

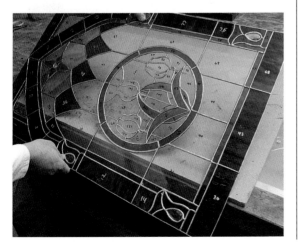

12 With the panel remaining vertical, carefully turn it around so that the unsoldered side faces you.

13 While lifting the panel with your top hand, secure the bottom with your other hand.

You will notice that all of the seams are filled with solder. This actually makes it easier to solder the back side, since you will only be using about half the amount of solder that was used on the front side.

14 Place the middle of the panel against the edge of the table and lower it onto the work board.

15 Flux the panel and apply a rounded bead of solder to the entire back side. Even though this side might not be viewed when displayed, complete it as carefully as you did the front side. You do not want those great-great-grandchildren being embarrassed over sloppy solder seams.

16 Turn the panel back over to the front side. Check to see if there are any places where solder has melted through from the back side. This will appear as a blob with the texture of your work board.

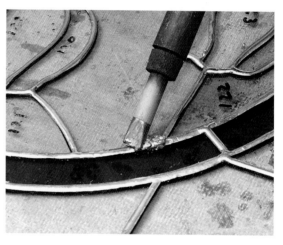

To correct these, apply a little flux and spread the extra solder around. The bigger the blob, the wider the area you should use to spread it out.

Framing the Panel

In order to dress up the edges and create a surface for mounting hooks to hang the panel, we will be attaching a metal border. Due to the size of the panel, lead, which is very soft, is not recommended. Copper can be used if you plan on using a copper-colored finish. Brass will work as well if you like that look. Since we will finish this panel with a black patina, zinc is our framing material of choice. It is rigid and will take a black patina as well. Zinc comes in several widths and we will use $^1/_2$ inch.

1 With a hacksaw or electric metal saw, cut two pieces of zinc about 1 inch long. One of these will be used to determine if there are areas where a solder buildup will prevent the zinc from slipping smoothly over the edge of the panel. Place the piece of zinc over the edge of the panel and run it around the entire panel.

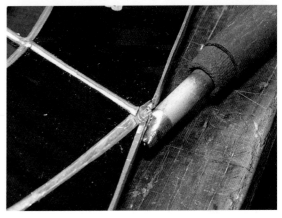

If you come to a seam where the solder is raised too high, flux the area lightly and melt off the solder.

2 Place the two 1-inch scrap pieces of zinc over the glass on the long sides of the panel, near the top.

3 Place a piece of zinc at least 24 inches long along the top of the panel, lining up evenly with one of the scrap pieces.

4 Draw a line on the zinc where it lines up with the other scrap piece.

5 Secure the zinc in a vice and cut it with your saw.

Check for proper fit. The strips of zinc will extend beyond the edges of the panel.

6 Repeat the process for a second strip of zinc that will go across the bottom of the panel.

7 Place both strips of zinc over the top and bottom edges of the panel and secure with flat nails.

8 Cut two long strips of zinc that fit between the pieces that are nailed in place and secure these with nails.

9 Flux all of the areas where solder seams from the panel meet the zinc strips, as well as the four corners.

10 To solder zinc, use the same temperatures settings as you did with soldering the panel. Unlike lead, zinc will not melt at that temperature.

Place the end of the solder at a point where a solder seam meets the zinc. Melt off approximately $1/8$ inch of solder. Lift the solder spool and lift the iron. Try not to move the iron along the zinc. Once solder is on the zinc, it cannot be removed.

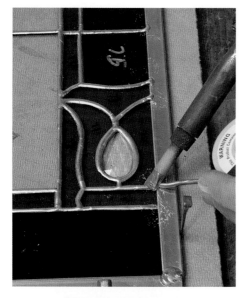

11 For the corners, lay the solder down on the seam, flatten your iron tip, and melt the solder. You will have to move your iron a little to create a fairly flat solder joint.

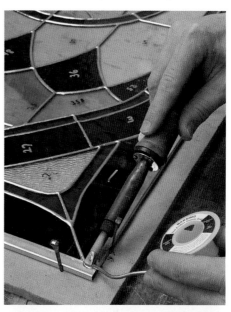

12 Turn the panel over as before; flux and solder the back side.

13 To solder the holes left at the corners, place the panel on one of its long sides, leaning it against the work table or wall.

Apply flux to each hole and fill it with solder. Use a sweeping motion as you pull melted solder across the hole. You will need to make several passes to fill the hole.

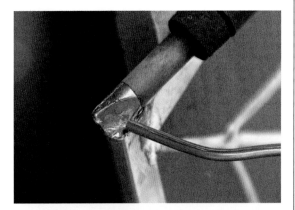

14 If you plan to free hang this panel, you will need to attach substantial hooks. Cut two 4-inch lengths of tinned copper wire, 14- or 16-gauge. If you have regular copper wire, apply flux and tin it first.

15 Bend each wire into a U-shape with the legs being about $^1/_4$ inch apart.

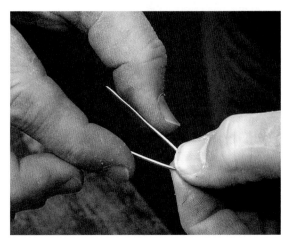

They should fit snugly over the zinc; position them about in the middle of the side pieces of the zinc frame.

16 Flux each top leg and the zinc below and solder them in place. Let your iron rest on the wire while the melting solder flows down to the zinc. This will create the firm bond that is needed to support the panel.

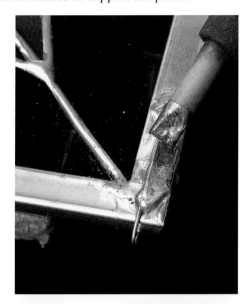

17 Turn the panel over and solder the other ends of the wire hooks.

Finishing the Panel

There are various chemicals that cause the metals on a stained glass panel to change color. Leaving the silver-colored solder unaltered is an option. If you decide to color the metals, several choices are available, including copper, pewter, antique brass, brown, and black. These patinas oxidize the raw metals, causing the change in color. We chose black for our panel. Two different patinas are necessary for the two metals.

Since the metal is being chemically treated, it must be perfectly clean to achieve maximum results.

1 With a sponge, clean the panel with the same cleaner you used before. The numbers will be easier to remove if you wet them with the cleaner and come back to them at the end.

2 Dry the panel with a towel.

3 Preparing the surface of the zinc requires a bit more work. With a ball of fine-grit steel wool, rub the zinc channel using a somewhat vigorous back-and-forth motion. This should produce a shiny surface on the zinc.

4 Remove the wool shavings with a bench brush.

5 To be sure that you are getting the panel clean, spray or wipe on a liberal amount of flux/patina remover. Buff this dry with a clean cloth or towel.

Note: Because of the chemical makeup of various patinas, you *must* wear rubber gloves to protect yourself—no shortcuts here.

6 Start with the black patina for zinc. Using a piece of soft sponge (we use old carpet padding), rub the patina back and forth on the zinc, being generous with the patina. Be sure to color the outside edges also.

7 Set the zinc patina and sponge aside until you do the other side.

With black patina for solder and a new sponge, rub all of the solder seams; again, be generous with the patina. Try to avoid getting it on the zinc.

10 Apply the flux/patina remover again and buff the panel dry. Sprinkle finishing wax around the panel and spread it out with a soft dry cloth (an old diaper works well).

8 Repeat the patina steps on the other side.

9 Rinse off the patina. With the same glass cleaner as before, go over the panel lightly and rinse again. Dry thoroughly.

11 Fold the cloth so you have a clean area and buff all the glass and metal to a pleasing shine.

Guess what? That was the last step. You are finished! Try to find a window to set it in so you can take a first look at your newly completed project.

If you are like the large majority of our students, you are probably somewhere between generally pleased and very pleased. Bear in mind two things: You will get better with practice, and you are developing advanced skills in a wonderful art form. The great-great-grandkids will be proud!

PRO TIP ✔

Even with what seems like a perfect cleaning, some areas of the zinc might not be colored well. It is more difficult to render a deep and even patina color on zinc than on solder.

With steel wool, scratch off most of the patina in areas where it is mottled or doesn't cover evenly. Reapply the patina for zinc and let it dry for a few minutes. Rinse and dry it as before.

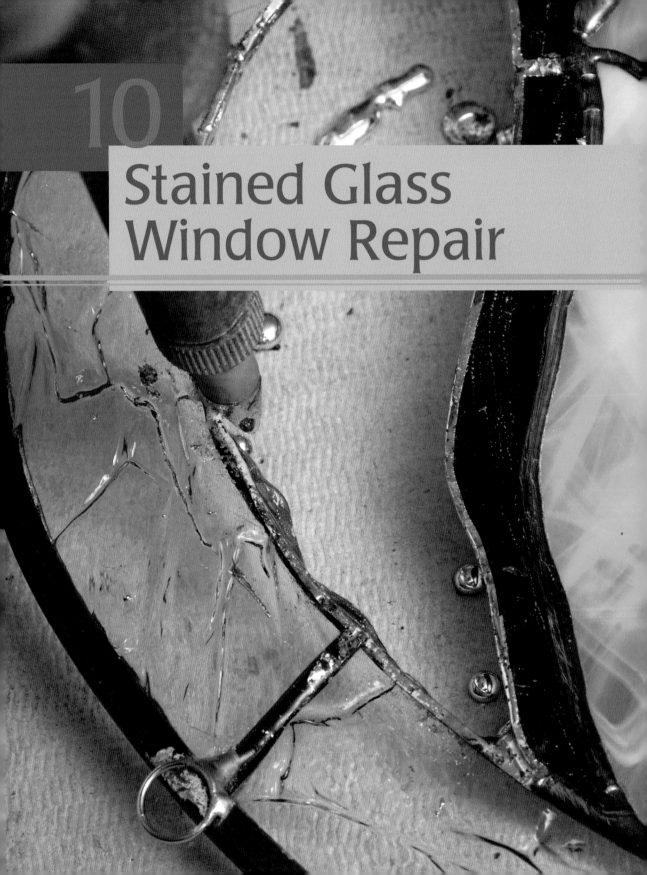

Stained Glass Window Repair

WHETHER IT HAPPENS SOONER OR LATER, BE assured that if you are involved with stained glass for any length of time, you will experience the inconvenience of a cracked piece of glass in one of your projects. We refer to this as an inconvenience—not catastrophe, not a big problem, not the end of the world—because, as you will see, it is not too difficult to replace the broken glass.

The processes are quite different for lead came panels and copper foil panels. Detailed instructions follow for both situations.

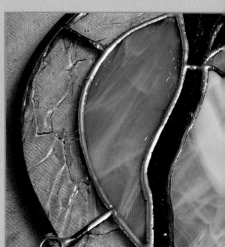

171

Repairing a Lead Came Panel

The wood-framed panel pictured below is an antique window, probably from the early 1900's. It has lightly seeded glass throughout the interior and is bordered by a bit darker amber colored glass with a hammered texture. Three mouth-blown roundels are located in the top section. The came throughout the window is $1/4$-inch H-lead. We will show you how to replace broken glass without removing the panel from the wood sash.

Lead is a relatively soft and malleable metal, the reason it is used for building stained glass windows. This also aids in the repair process.

1   With a utility knife, scrape the cement that holds the broken piece. The powder that you see is dried-up cement (Remember: this panel is eighty years old or so). Scrape lightly so you do not gouge the back of the lead. You might have to scrape several times on each side, depending on the condition of the cement. The object is to loosen the cement, not necessarily to remove all of it.

2 With a marker, draw lines from each corner of the triangle to the middle of the opposite side. Draw several additional lines as shown.

3 Score all of the lines, being careful not to let your cutter run onto the other pieces of glass.

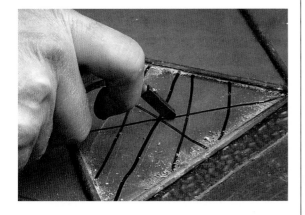

4 Turn the panel over and scrape out cement on that side.

5 With the brass ball on your cutter, gently tap on all score lines, causing the glass to crack.

Continue tapping until several shards of glass are pushed out onto the work table.

6 Lay the panel flat or hold it vertically and remove the remaining shards of glass by wiggling each one back and forth until they are loose. These shards are very sharp, so be careful!

7 With a stiff pointed instrument such as a horseshoe nail or the point of a lead knife, remove any remaining cement or glass pieces.

If small pieces are wedged in the lead, use needle-nose pliers to free them.

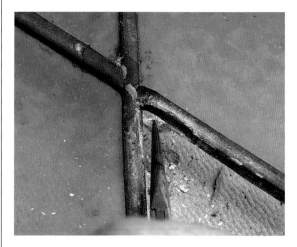

8 Position your lead knife inside the opening and cut halfway through the lead joint in each of the corners. Use a back-and-forth rocking motion to penetrate the lead and only cut the top edge.

Now we will bend the top leaf of two sides to fit in the replacement glass.

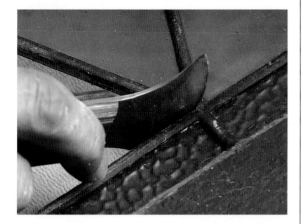

9 Using a wooden or plastic fid or other flat tool, make a pass along the underside of the lead, pushing it up a little as you go.

Repeat several times, changing the angle of the tool a little bit during each pass. Do this process gradually to avoid creasing the lead too much.

10 Repeat the same steps for the second side of the opening.

The object is to raise each leaf about 75 degrees—bending the lead straight up (90 degrees) is too much.

11 Take a piece of replacement glass and set it up on the opening. Place it about $1/16$ inch over the inside edge of the lead that is not bent.

12 Now trace the replacement piece along the two other sides of the triangle. The lines should be just inside the opening of the bent lead.

13 Cut the glass on the lines.

14 Slide the bottom edge of the glass into the unopened came and tilt it forward until it rests flat on the bottom edges of the two opened leads. You might have to grind the glass to fit or open the leads a little more.

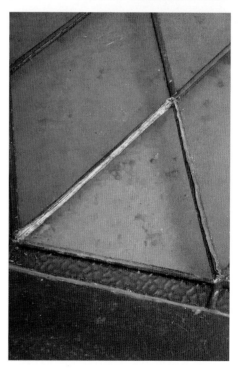

15 Support the glass from the back side so the panel does not flex and run the fid along the bent leads to flatten them out again. Bend the leads gradually. You may need to make several passes. Stop the bending before the leads actually touch the glass.

16 Mix up a golf-ball-sized amount of cement with the consistency of modeling clay. If it is runny, add some whiting until you can form a ball.

17 Push the cement under all the cames, cleaning off the excess as you go.

18 Sprinkle whiting across the piece and scrub with a stiff, natural bristle brush.

19 Repeat the cementing steps on the reverse side.

The repair is finished.

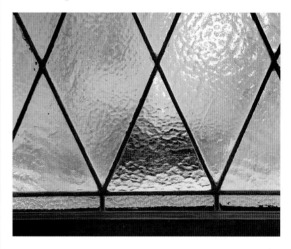

Repairing a Copper Foil Panel

Lots of things can cause glass to break in a foiled panel. Several of my "inconveniences" have been the result of:

- Dropping the solder spool
- Too much heat
- Bumping the finished panel on the metal sink
- Leaning on the project
- Unknown and mysterious reasons

Whatever the cause, the repair process is the same. And remember that intangible: patience. Take your time or you might do further damage.

1 Draw a tic-tac-toe grid on the broken piece.

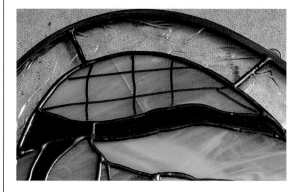

2 Using a back-and-forth scrubbing motion with fine steel wool, scratch off the patina on both sides of the panel.

3 Score the grid lines.

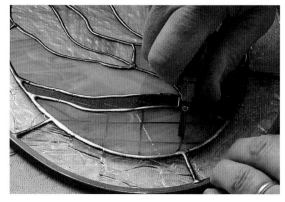

4 Turn the panel over and with the brass screw on the end of your cutter, tap along the back of all the grid lines, causing them to crack.

5 Continue tapping until several of the middle pieces are completely pushed out.

6 Apply flux to the seams around the broken piece.

7 Melt the solder where one of the pieces of glass is attached to the foil. Using needle-nose pliers in your opposite hand, take hold of that piece and lightly pull it loose. Do not tug too hard—just wait until the adhesive from the foil begins to melt.

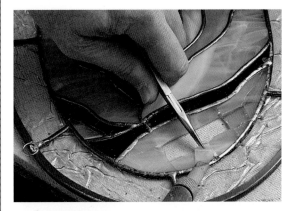

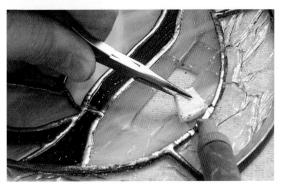

8 Repeat for all the remaining glass pieces.

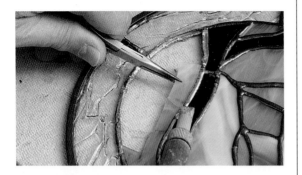

9 Locate the seam where the ends of the foil from the broken piece overlapped. Melt the solder in this area and flick one of the ends with the iron so that you can take hold of it with your pliers.

10 Continue slowly melting the solder while gently separating the foil from the adjoining pieces. Pulling too hard can result in the foil from the adjoining pieces coming loose.

11 Hold the panel an inch or so above the work board. Flux the seam and melt off the remaining solder, allowing it to drop onto the surface.

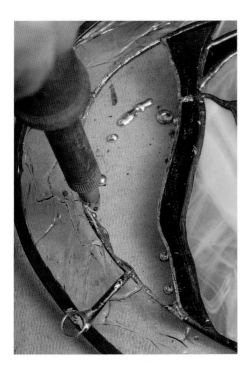

NOTE: The opening should be very smooth without any solder build up.

12 Place a piece of replacement glass under the panel and adjust it for the proper grain direction. Trace a new piece.

13 Cut the piece in the middle of the pattern line. This will allow for the foil.

14 Check for proper fit and grind as necessary. There should be a little movement to allow for the foil.

15 Wash and foil the glass. Flux the opening and the new glass.

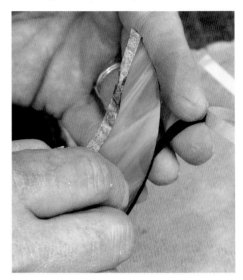

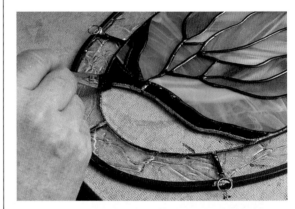

16
Fit the glass and tack solder it into place.

17
Finish soldering on both sides.

18
Wash the repaired area, and finish it as you did originally.

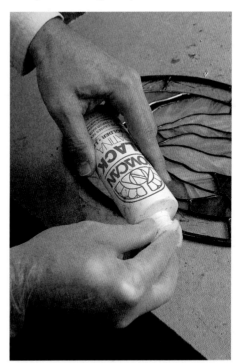

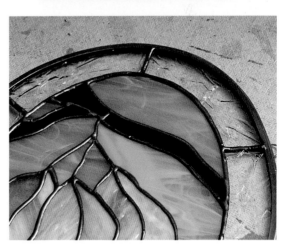

11

Building a Wooden Frame

THE LEADED PANEL THAT WE FINISHED IN Chapter 8 weighs around 15 pounds. That, coupled with the fact that the lead is soft and will stretch, makes it unwise to hang it from hooks that are soldered onto the edges. This chapter will show you how to put together a handsome oak frame from readily available wood stock. For this project, you will need two 6-foot-long pieces of pregrooved oak that are $1^{3}/_{8}$-inch wide and a four-piece set of oak corner brackets.

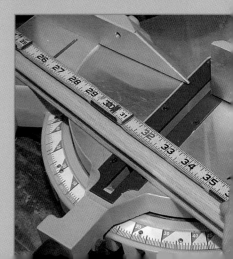

1 Measure the height of the leaded panel on both ends as well as in the middle. If there is any variation, choose the longest measurement. Our panel measures $33^1/_4$ inches.

2 Now add 2 inches and mark this measurement on both of your boards. Cut the wood with a hand or miter saw.

3 Remove any rough spots with sandpaper, and set the wood aside.

4 Measure the width of the panel at both ends and the middle. Ours measures $21^3/8$ inches. Take the longest measurement and subtract $3/4$ inch. Mark the two pieces of wood to be cut.

5 Now cut both pieces and sand.

6 The four frame sides should be dry-fitted into the corner brackets to be sure they fit properly.

Take one of the long sides and push brackets firmly onto both ends.

building a wooden frame • **189**

7 Insert the short sides into the same brackets. Make sure they fit snugly.

8 Slide the panel into the three-sided frame.

9 Push both ends of the remaining long side into the two remaining brackets.

10 Align the brackets with the two short boards and push them together.

11 Decide if you want to paint or stain the wood frame. We chose a clear oil stain to accentuate the beautiful grain in the oak.

12 Disassemble the frame parts.

13 Using an old rag, rub the stain on all four sides and the brackets (if you are using paint, a paintbrush is recommended).

14 Allow the stain or paint to dry per the directions from the manufacturer. Then put a small amount of wood glue on a piece of paper.

15 Using a clean brush, spread a layer of glue on all six surfaces inside two of the brackets.

16 Insert both ends of one of the long boards into the brackets.

17 Insert the two short sides into the same brackets.

18 Slide the leaded glass panel into the three-sided frame.

19 Apply glue in the remaining two brackets. Insert the other long side into both brackets. Align the brackets with the short sides and attach snugly.

20 Now you will screw the corner brackets to the four sides.

It is advisable to predrill the oak sides due to the hardness of the oak and the softness of the brass. Choose a drill bit that is smaller in diameter than the screw. You should be able to see the screw threads around the drill bit.

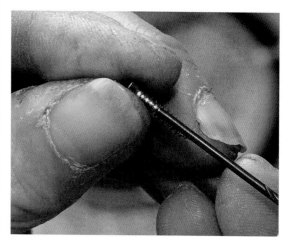

21 Locate the predrilled hole on the bracket and drill through into the oak side. The depth should be the length of the screw.

22 Using an old candle, wax the threads of the screw and attach it through the corner bracket into the oak side. Use a hand screwdriver and do not overtighten.

23 Repeat steps 21 and 22 for the other side of the bracket.

24 Repeat for the other three brackets.

25 Now you will need to attach the hangers below the brackets on the outside edges of both long sides.

Measure down 1 inch from the bottom of the bracket, hold the hanger in place, and put a pencil mark on the top hole.

26 Predrill the wood and attach the hanger with a screw. Remember to wax the screw.

27 Predrill the bottom hole and attach the screw.

28 Repeat steps 25, 26, and 27 for the second hanger.

12

Stained Glass
Panel Gallery

Antique leaded window, circa 1920.

From the book "Orchids in Glass" by Chantal Pare, Randy Wardell, editor. Fabricated by Leroy Summers using assorted art glasses.

Calla Lillies

Designed and fabricated by Lynn Haunstein.

Iris in Bloom
Designed and fabricated by Nan Maund.

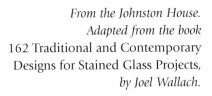

From the Flood home,
Harrisburg, Pennsylvania.

From the Johnston House.
Adapted from the book
162 Traditional and Contemporary
Designs for Stained Glass Projects,
by Joel Wallach.

Dichromatic Diamonds
Designed and fabricated by Rainbow Vision Stained Glass.

Vase Full of Irises

Designed and fabricated by Rainbow Vision Stained Glass.

Waiting for the Harvest
Designed and fabricated by Rainbow Vision Stained Glass.

Sunrise from the Cove
Designed and fabricated by Rainbow Vision Stained Glass.

Victorian Fleur
Designed and fabricated by Rainbow Vision Stained Glass.

Easter Cross

Designed and fabricated by Rainbow Vision Stained Glass. A modified version of this design is included as an option for the circular medallion in the large featured design.

resources

Books

Berkery, Dennis. 2002. *300 Stained Glass Cabinet Door Designs.* Madison, WI: The Vinery Stained Glass Studio.

Gibbs, Leslie. 2002. *Tropical Breezes.* Olympia, WA: CKE Publications.

Relei, Carolyn. 1990. *Decorative Doorways Stained Glass Pattern Book.* New York: Dover Publications.

Wallach, Joel. 1974. *162 Traditional and Contempory Designs for Stained Glass Projects.* New York: Dover Publications.

Online

Glastar Corp.
20721 Marilla Street
Chatsworth, CA 91311
800-423-5635
www.glastar.com
Manufacturer of glass grinders and other stained glass tools. This site includes lots of glass-related topics.

Inland Craft Products, Co.
32052 Edward Drive
Madison Heights, MI 48071
800-521-8428
www.inlandcraft.com
Carries glass grinders and other equipment used in stained glass. The website also includes a handy state-by-state locator of stained glass supply stores.

Kokomo Opalescent Glass
1310 South Market Street
Kokomo, IN 46904-2265
765-457-8136
www.kog.com
The oldest glass manufacturer in the country, established in 1888. Take a virtual tour of the factory, click on their sample set, and see products from their hot glass studio.

Odyssey Lamps
8317 Secura Way
Santa Fe Springs, CA 90670
800-4031981
www.odysseylamps.com
This website shows the many molds and patterns available as well as prices and other interesting information.

Rainbow Vision Stained Glass
3105 Walnut Street
Harrisburg, PA 17109
800-762-9309
www.rainbowvisionsg.com
Contains information about all things stained glass; equipment and materials are available for purchase. Full-size patterns for boxes, lamps, and panels. Send a photo of your completed project for inclusion in the gallery.

Retailers of Art Glass and Supplies (RAGS)
www.stainedglassretailers.com
A nonprofit organization of owners of retail stores selling stained glass supplies around the world. Includes good information about the craft, as well as listings of supplier locations.

Spectrum Glass
24105 Sno-Woodinville Road
Woodinville, WA 98072
425-483-6699
www.spectrumglass.com
This site is loaded with technical information, sample colors, free patterns, and much more.

Uroboros Glass
2139 North Kerby Avenue
Portland, OR 97227
503-284-4900
www.uroboros.com
This site includes details about the factory and glass samples.

Wissmach Glass, Co.
420 Stephen Street
Paden City, WV 26159
304-337-2253
www.wissmachglass.com
This site has factory information, glass samples, and a gallery.

Worden Lamps
PO Box 519
Granger, WA 98932
800-541-1103
www.wordensystem.com
This website displays the many molds and patterns available and other related products.

Youghiogheny Glass
900 West Crawford Avenue
Connellsville, PA 15425
724-628-0332
www.youghioghenyglass.com
Established in 1978, this company specializes in Tiffany reproduction glass. This site includes sample sets, gallery, and factory information.

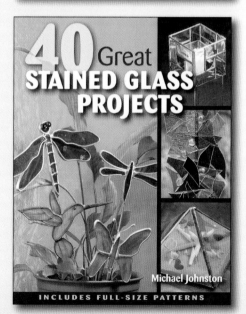

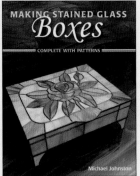
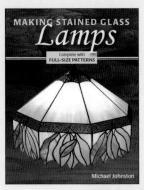

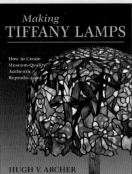

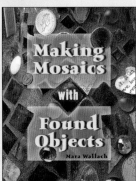